MAJOR WORLD LEADERS

MAJOR WORLD LEADERS

Gerhard Schroeder

Kerry Acker

CHELSEA HOUSE
PUBLISHERS
A Haights Cross Communications Company

Philadelphia

CHELSEA HOUSE PUBLISHERS

V.P., New Product Development Sally Cheney
Director of Production Kim Shinners
Creative Manager Takeshi Takahashi
Manufacturing Manager Diann Grasse

Staff for GERHARD SCHROEDER

Executive Editor Lee Marcott
Senior Editor Tara Koellhoffer
Production Editor Megan Emery
Picture Research 21st Century Publishing and Communications, Inc.
Series and Cover Designer Takeshi Takahashi
Layout 21st Century Publishing and Communications, Inc.

A Haights Cross Communications ✈ Company

http://www.chelseahouse.com

First Printing

1 3 5 7 9 8 6 4 2

Library of Congress Cataloging-in-Publication Data

Acker, Kerry.
  Gerhard Schroeder / by Kerry Acker.
     p. cm. -- (Major world leaders)
Summary: A biography of Chancellor Gerhard Schroeder, twentieth-century German
politician. Includes index.
  ISBN 0-7910-7652-0
  1. Schrèoder, Gerhard, 1944---Juvenile literature. 2. Prime ministers--Germany--
Biography--Juvenile literature. 3. Politicians--Germany--Biography--Juvenile litera-
ture. [1. Schrèoder, Gerhard, 1944- 2. Prime ministers. 3. Politicians.] I. Title. II.
Series.
  DD290.33.S37A25 2003
  943.088'2'092--dc22

                                                              2003013674

TABLE OF CONTENTS

On Leadership

Arthur M. Schlesinger, jr.

Leadership, it may be said, is really what makes the world go round. Love no doubt smoothes the passage; but love is a private transaction between consenting adults. Leadership is a public transaction with history. The idea of leadership affirms the capacity of individuals to move, inspire, and mobilize masses of people so that they act together in pursuit of an end. Sometimes leadership serves good purposes, sometimes bad; but whether the end is benign or evil, great leaders are those men and women who leave their personal stamp on history.

Now, the very concept of leadership implies the proposition that individuals can make a difference. This proposition has never been universally accepted. From classical times to the present day, eminent thinkers have regarded individuals as no more than the agents and pawns of larger forces, whether the gods and goddesses of the ancient world or, in the modern era, race, class, nation, the dialectic, the will of the people, the spirit of the times, history itself. Against such forces, the individual dwindles into insignificance.

So contends the thesis of historical determinism. Tolstoy's great novel *War and Peace* offers a famous statement of the case. Why, Tolstoy asked, did millions of men in the Napoleonic Wars, denying their human feelings and their common sense, move back and forth across Europe slaughtering their fellows? "The war," Tolstoy answered, "was bound to happen simply because it was bound to happen." All prior history determined it. As for leaders, they, Tolstoy said, "are but the labels that serve to give a name to an end and, like labels, they have the least possible connection with the event." The greater the leader, "the more conspicuous the inevitability and the predestination of every act he commits." The leader, said Tolstoy, is "the slave of history."

Determinism takes many forms. Marxism is the determinism of class. Nazism the determinism of race. But the idea of men and women as the slaves of history runs athwart the deepest human instincts. Rigid determinism abolishes the idea of human freedom—the assumption of free choice that underlies every move we make, every word we speak, every thought we think. It abolishes the idea of human responsibility, since it is manifestly unfair to reward or punish people for actions that are by definition beyond their control. No one can live consistently by any deterministic creed. The Marxist states prove this themselves by their extreme susceptibility to the cult of leadership.

More than that, history refutes the idea that individuals make no difference. In December 1931 a British politician crossing Fifth Avenue in New York City between 76th and 77th Streets around 10:30 P.M. looked in the wrong direction and was knocked down by an automobile—a moment, he later recalled, of a man aghast, a world aglare: "I do not understand why I was not broken like an eggshell or squashed like a gooseberry." Fourteen months later an American politician, sitting in an open car in Miami, Florida, was fired on by an assassin; the man beside him was hit. Those who believe that individuals make no difference to history might well ponder whether the next two decades would have been the same had Mario Constasino's car killed Winston Churchill in 1931 and Giuseppe Zangara's bullet killed Franklin Roosevelt in 1933. Suppose, in addition, that Lenin had died of typhus in Siberia in 1895 and that Hitler had been killed on the Western Front in 1916. What would the 20th century have looked like now?

For better or for worse, individuals do make a difference. "The notion that a people can run itself and its affairs anonymously," wrote the philosopher William James, "is now well known to be the silliest of absurdities. Mankind does nothing save through initiatives on the part of inventors, great or small, and imitation by the rest of us—these are the sole factors in human progress. Individuals of genius show the way, and set the patterns, which common people then adopt and follow."

Leadership, James suggests, means leadership in thought as well as in action. In the long run, leaders in thought may well make the greater difference to the world. "The ideas of economists and political philosophers, both when they are right and when they are wrong," wrote John Maynard Keynes, "are more powerful than is commonly understood. Indeed the world is ruled by little else. Practical men, who believe themselves to be quite exempt from any intellectual influences, are usually the slaves of some defunct economist. . . . The power of vested interests is vastly exaggerated compared with the gradual encroachment of ideas."

But, as Woodrow Wilson once said, "Those only are leaders of men, in the general eye, who lead in action.... It is at their hands that new thought gets its translation into the crude language of deeds." Leaders in thought often invent in solitude and obscurity, leaving to later generations the tasks of imitation. Leaders in action—the leaders portrayed in this series—have to be effective in their own time.

And they cannot be effective by themselves. They must act in response to the rhythms of their age. Their genius must be adapted, in a phrase from William James, "to the receptivities of the moment." Leaders are useless without followers. "There goes the mob," said the French politician, hearing a clamor in the streets. "I am their leader. I must follow them." Great leaders turn the inchoate emotions of the mob to purposes of their own. They seize on the opportunities of their time, the hopes, fears, frustrations, crises, potentialities. They succeed when events have prepared the way for them, when the community is awaiting to be aroused, when they can provide the clarifying and organizing ideas. Leadership completes the circuit between the individual and the mass and thereby alters history.

It may alter history for better or for worse. Leaders have been responsible for the most extravagant follies and most monstrous crimes that have beset suffering humanity. They have also been vital in such gains as humanity has made in individual freedom, religious and racial tolerance, social justice, and respect for human rights.

There is no sure way to tell in advance who is going to lead for good and who for evil. But a glance at the gallery of men and women in MAJOR WORLD LEADERS suggests some useful tests.

One test is this: Do leaders lead by force or by persuasion? By command or by consent? Through most of history leadership was exercised by the divine right of authority. The duty of followers was to defer and to obey. "Theirs not to reason why/Theirs but to do and die." On occasion, as with the so-called enlightened despots of the 18th century in Europe, absolutist leadership was animated by humane purposes. More often, absolutism nourished the passion for domination, land, gold, and conquest and resulted in tyranny.

The great revolution of modern times has been the revolution of equality. "Perhaps no form of government," wrote the British historian James Bryce in his study of the United States, *The American Commonwealth*, "needs great leaders so much as democracy." The idea that all people should be equal in their legal condition has undermined the old structure of authority, hierarchy, and deference. The revolution of equality has had two contrary effects on the nature of leadership. For equality, as Alexis de Tocqueville pointed out in his great study *Democracy in America*, might mean equality in servitude as well as equality in freedom.

"I know of only two methods of establishing equality in the political world," Tocqueville wrote. "Rights must be given to every citizen, or none at all to anyone . . . save one, who is the master of all." There was no middle ground "between the sovereignty of all and the absolute power of one man." In his astonishing prediction of 20th-century totalitarian dictatorship, Tocqueville explained how the revolution of equality could lead to the *Führerprinzip* and more terrible absolutism than the world had ever known.

But when rights are given to every citizen and the sovereignty of all is established, the problem of leadership takes a new form, becomes more exacting than ever before. It is easy to issue commands and enforce them by the rope and the stake, the concentration camp and the *gulag*. It is much harder to use argument and achievement to overcome opposition and win consent. The Founding Fathers of the United States understood the difficulty. They believed that history had given them the opportunity to decide, as Alexander Hamilton wrote in the first Federalist Paper, whether men are indeed capable of basing government on "reflection and choice, or whether they are forever destined to depend . . . on accident and force."

Government by reflection and choice called for a new style of leadership and a new quality of followership. It required leaders to be responsive to popular concerns, and it required followers to be active and informed participants in the process. Democracy does not eliminate emotion from politics; sometimes it fosters demagoguery; but it is confident that, as the greatest of democratic leaders put it, you cannot fool all of the people all of the time. It measures leadership by results and retires those who overreach or falter or fail.

It is true that in the long run despots are measured by results too. But they can postpone the day of judgment, sometimes indefinitely, and in the meantime they can do infinite harm. It is also true that democracy is no guarantee of virtue and intelligence in government, for the voice of the people is not necessarily the voice of God. But democracy, by assuring the right of opposition, offers built-in resistance to the evils inherent in absolutism. As the theologian Reinhold Niebuhr summed it up, "Man's capacity for justice makes democracy possible, but man's inclination to justice makes democracy necessary."

A second test for leadership is the end for which power is sought. When leaders have as their goal the supremacy of a master race or the promotion of totalitarian revolution or the acquisition and exploitation of colonies or the protection of greed and privilege or the preservation of personal power, it is likely that their leadership will do little to advance the cause of humanity. When their goal is the abolition of slavery, the liberation of women, the enlargement of opportunity for the poor and powerless, the extension of equal rights to racial minorities, the defense of the freedoms of expression and opposition, it is likely that their leadership will increase the sum of human liberty and welfare.

Leaders have done great harm to the world. They have also conferred great benefits. You will find both sorts in this series. Even "good" leaders must be regarded with a certain wariness. Leaders are not demigods; they put on their trousers one leg after another just like ordinary mortals. No leader is infallible, and every leader needs to be reminded of this at regular intervals. Irreverence irritates leaders but is their salvation. Unquestioning submission corrupts leaders and demeans followers. Making a cult of a leader is always a mistake. Fortunately hero worship generates its own antidote. "Every hero," said Emerson, "becomes a bore at last."

The signal benefit the great leaders confer is to embolden the rest of us to live according to our own best selves, to be active, insistent, and resolute in affirming our own sense of things. For great leaders attest to the reality of human freedom against the supposed inevitabilities of history. And they attest to the wisdom and power that may lie within the most unlikely of us, which is why Abraham Lincoln remains the supreme example of great leadership. A great leader, said Emerson, exhibits new possibilities to all humanity. "We feed on genius. . . . Great men exist that there may be greater men."

Great leaders, in short, justify themselves by emancipating and empowering their followers. So humanity struggles to master its destiny, remembering with Alexis de Tocqueville: "It is true that around every man a fatal circle is traced beyond which he cannot pass; but within the wide verge of that circle he is powerful and free; as it is with man, so with communities." ∎

1

Defying the United States

G erhard Schroeder's chancellorship was not in good shape in the late summer of 2002. A member of the Social Democratic Party, Schroeder was up for reelection, and for several months in the polls he had been trailing behind his conservative opponent, Edmund Stoiber, premier of the state of Bavaria and member of the Christian Democratic Union–Christian Social Union coalition. This was largely due to the miserable state of the economy. Germany was heading into its second recession in just over a year. Unemployment was nearing its highest point in the post–World War II era (almost 4.1 million people were out of work), and the extravagant social-support system to which Germans were so accustomed was moving toward collapse. Labor costs remained incredibly high, and Schroeder's economic packages had been insufficient to thoroughly solve the nation's economic woes. Schroeder had also failed to fulfill his pledge to create

German Chancellor Gerhard Schroeder gives the victory sign as he addresses a campaign rally in July 2002. Schroeder was up for reelection that coming September.

more jobs. During his first campaign for chancellor, he had said, "He who, after four years, does not reduce the number of job seekers to 3.5 million or less, will neither be re-elected nor will he be worthy of being so."

Schroeder, who campaigned for his first election as a proponent of what he called "the new middle"—a pragmatic, modern brand of politics that favors the free market yet is concerned with social justice—had successfully passed the most extensive tax reform package in German history during his term. He had also improved relations with Russia and, supported by his Green Party coalition partners, had implemented a new immigration policy and negotiated a plan to phase out Germany's 19 nuclear power plants. From the start, though, Schroeder was criticized for his opportunism and his apparent tendency to change his mind to accommodate different constituents. Once known as the "comrade of the bosses," he often aligned himself with big business, yet occasionally switched allegiances and backed the trade unions, the rank-and-file of his Social Democratic Party. Each side often felt he did not have the courage to stand up to the other.

In international affairs, too, it was difficult to distinguish where Schroeder's true loyalties lay. He started off by cozying up to British Prime Minister Tony Blair, his partner in left-of-center politics, but then he seemed to concentrate more on bolstering his relationship with France. France and Germany had long enjoyed a special alliance; together they were known as "the engine" of Europe. That relationship, however, has been less than consistent and has suffered considerably, in part because of differences over the future of Europe.

Schroeder and U.S. President George W. Bush had disagreed on issues such as the Kyoto Protocol. (Bush did not back this treaty, signed by 99 nations, which would reduce greenhouse-gas emissions.) At first, they disagreed on Bush's controversial multibillion-dollar missile-defense system; however, in another case of switching sides, Schroeder eventually accepted it. But despite their disagreements, the two leaders initially seemed to get along fine.

In 2002, however, when Schroeder was campaigning for reelection, the traditionally strong U.S.-German bond was severely damaged. Although Germany sent troops to Afghanistan in November 2001 to participate in Bush's "war on terror," Schroeder faced much opposition at home—from members of his own party, from several of his Green Party coalition partners, and from many German voters. When Bush began to talk about broadening his "war on terror" to include Saddam Hussein's regime in Iraq, Schroeder expressed his skepticism. As Bush became more open about the need for a "regime change" in Iraq, Schroeder's rhetoric against American intervention intensified. Germany, a country where many have a deep-seated revulsion to war, responded with tremendous support for its chancellor. His approval ratings skyrocketed.

While Bush fought to get the United Nations (UN) to support military action in Iraq, Schroeder rejected the proposal unconditionally. When he declared at a campaign rally and in a televised debate that he wholeheartedly rejected what he called "any American adventures in Iraq," German crowds erupted in applause. He said, "I warn against talk of war and military action. Those who are making plans for such action should have a political framework for doing so." Schroeder's opposition to war was just the boost he needed to regain his popularity in Germany. Many critics accused Schroeder of exploiting the issue and the pacifist attitudes of German voters to win the election.

Schroeder's decision to defy the United States was risky, though. Many conservative older Germans felt historically indebted to the United States and the North Atlantic Treaty Organization (NATO). Schroeder's antiwar stance also jeopardized his relationship with many members of the European Union (EU), such as Great Britain, which backed Bush's plan. He risked isolating Germany within the EU.

Most of all, however, Schroeder's aggressive tone and language created serious hostility between the United States and Germany. This problem only got worse when, three days before the election, German justice minister Herta Daeubler-Gmelin compared the American president to former German dictator Adolf Hitler. She said that, like Hitler, Bush was using war to distract Americans from domestic difficulties.

Schroeder apparently believed that the relationship between Germany and the United States was strong enough to withstand his campaign rhetoric, but he immediately sent a written apology to Bush (and did not keep Daubler-Gmelin in his cabinet during his next term). Still, it seemed the gesture was too little, too late. Condoleeza Rice, the U.S. national security advisor, said that Schroeder had "poisoned" the German-American alliance.

Schroeder did win reelection, but Bush did not call to congratulate him, as had typically been done in the past. Never in the history of modern Germany had a chancellor spoken so brazenly against one of the nation's greatest allies. Schroeder was left to repair the damage he had done to the German-American relationship, in addition to tackling enormous economic problems in his own country.

2

A Future Chancellor in Struggling Germany, 1930–1964

At the onset of the 1930s, Germany was in a severe economic crisis. Massive unemployment, business closings, and high inflation crippled the Weimar Republic, the popular name ascribed to the government after the so-called Weimar Constitution was drafted in 1919 following World War I. Europe and the United States were in the grip of a worldwide depression, and war reparations Germany was required to pay only added to the nation's financial

The most notorious chancellor in German history was Adolf Hitler, seen here in a 1937 photograph. Hitler seized ultimate power over the nation and began a systematic extermination of Jews and other ethnic groups he considered inferior.

distress. Thousands of hungry and out-of-work Germans lined up at soup kitchens across the country.

Dissatisfied with the Weimar government and desperate to escape their poverty, German voters embraced some radical political parties, like the Communists and the National Socialist German Workers' Party, better known as the Nazis. In January 1933, Adolf Hitler, the leader of the Nazis, became chancellor. He rose to prominence in part by promising to restore Germany's reputation as a strong nation. He held extreme nationalist and racist views, and placed the blame for Germany's economic woes squarely on the Jewish people and other minorities.

Once he became chancellor, Hitler made himself dictator and swiftly established a totalitarian state, the Third Reich, in which all political opposition was brutally suppressed. The Nazis outlawed elections, controlled the media, restricted personal liberties, and tolerated no political dissent. The Gestapo (the Nazi secret police) and the SS (*Schutzstaffel*, the Nazi militia) ruthlessly enforced this policy of intolerance, and all sectors of German society were forced (in a program called *Gleichschaltung*, or "synchronization") to support Hitler and the Nazi Party. Young people between the ages of 10 and 18 were required to join the Hitler Youth movement (the *Hitlerjugend*), a semi-military organization.

The Third Reich soon opened concentration camps for political dissenters and people the Nazis deemed undesirable. In all, about 26 million people were imprisoned in these horrifying places. Prisoners were put to work, and if they were physically unable to perform the hard labor, they were often killed. In many camps, the Nazis tortured prisoners and eventually put forth their program of mass extermination, in which they massacred Jews and others they considered racially or socially inferior. Between 1933 and 1945, a period known as the Holocaust, the Nazis slaughtered more than 6 million European Jews and about 6 million members of other ethnic groups in concentration camps.

Hitler allied himself with other dictators—Italy's Benito Mussolini and Spain's Francisco Franco. He aggressively pursued territorial expansion, annexing Austria in 1938 and occupying Czechoslovakia in 1939. After German tanks and bombers moved into Poland in 1939, however, Great Britain and France declared war on Germany, thus beginning World War II, a bloody and costly global conflict that was ultimately responsible for the deaths of some 55 million people. By 1940, German forces had conquered Denmark, Norway, Belgium, the Netherlands, and France. By 1941, Germany had conducted a massive bombing campaign of British cities (the Blitz), killing at least 40,000 people (mostly civilians). The Germans also invaded the Soviet Union and formed an alliance (the Axis powers) with Japan and Italy.

After the Japanese bombed the American naval base at Pearl Harbor, Hawaii, the United States entered the war, joining with Britain and the Soviet Union to form the Allies. By 1942, Germany and the Axis powers were starting to lose ground.

This was the state of the world when Gerhard Fritz Kurt Schroeder, the future chancellor of the Federal Republic of Germany, was born on April 7, 1944. His mother, Erika, gave birth to Gerhard, her second child, in the village of Mossenberg, in Lower Saxony, Germany, a region characterized by large swaths of farmland and significant reserves of iron and oil. Soon after Gerhard was born, his father, Fritz, died while fighting for German forces on the eastern front in Romania. Lance Corporal Schroeder never saw his son.

THE POSTWAR YEARS

By April 1945, German cities had been devastated by a sweeping Allied bombing campaign, and Hitler, watching his country collapse, committed suicide in his Berlin bunker while Soviets pummeled the city. By May 1945, the Allies had defeated the Nazis in Europe; three months later, after the United States dropped atomic bombs on the cities of Hiroshima and Nagasaki, the Japanese also surrendered. World War II, the most devastating war in history, was finally over.

In 1945 and 1946, the Nuremberg Trials brought to justice those accused of war crimes. A military tribunal, set up by the United States, Britain, France, and the Soviet Union, sentenced several Nazi leaders to death and sent many others to prison.

The question of what to do with Germany, a country in ruins, was resolved when the Allied powers divided the land

After World War II ended, Germany—and the city of Berlin itself—was divided among the victorious Allied powers to be reorganized and governed. In this 1949 photograph, a British driver is being detained at a Soviet-American boundary checkpoint in Berlin.

into four zones, each controlled by one of the four countries that won the war: the United States, Great Britain, France, and the Soviet Union. Tensions between the Soviet Union and the other three nations prevented the unification of the occupied zones. So, in 1949, the American, French, and British combined their zones to form a parliamentary republic, the Federal Republic of Germany (West Germany), with Bonn as its capital. West Germany, with a population of about 50 million people, adopted capitalist economic programs and military structures similar to those prevalent in Western nations. The Soviet-occupied area became known as the German Democratic Republic (East Germany), which became part of the Communist bloc with other Central and Eastern European nations. The population of East Germany was about 17 million. The city of Berlin was also divided, and the eastern section became the capital of East Germany.

During the postwar years, world politics shifted dramatically as the Soviet Union and the United States emerged as the two new superpowers. The Soviet Union presided over the Communist Eastern bloc countries, while the United States headed the capitalist Western bloc. Until 1990, the two nations were engaged in what was called the Cold War, an ideological and economic rivalry marked most significantly by the rapid stockpiling of powerful weapons and the threat of nuclear war. The Cold War dictated practically all international political affairs until both sides began to disarm in the late 1980s.

YOUNG GERHARD

From 1945 to 1947, West Germany experienced a severe food shortage, caused primarily by a struggling economy and bad harvests. The situation grew more urgent when 10 million ethnic German refugees arrived from Eastern Europe. Erika and Fritz Schroeder had been impoverished when Fritz was alive, but after his death Erika had to feed and shelter her two children on her own. In 1947, Erika married an unskilled worker named Paul Vosseler. The marriage produced Schroeder's three half siblings before Vosseler died of tuberculosis in 1964.

Young Gerhard's mother, whom Schroeder affectionately called "the lioness," took five cleaning jobs at once to feed her five small children. One of the jobs involved cleaning the barracks of British occupation forces in the town of Lemgo, in northern Germany. Schroeder has said, "We were literally as poor as church mice."

Schroeder once admitted that he was the scruffy boy with whom other children would refuse to play. He did shine as an elementary school student, however, showing promise as an articulate speaker and a capable debater. He also learned the value of hard work at a young age. When he was around 12, he spent the summer toiling in fields, picking potatoes to help feed and clothe his younger siblings. At age 14, he was forced to quit school—he was, in essence, the father figure of the family, and therefore had to assume the role of breadwinner. While his class-mates furthered their studies at *gymnasium* (secondary school), young Gerhard set off to look for work. He has said, "It makes a difference," in reference to his mother's not having enough money for his schooling. "That's a decision that affects your life."

TEEN YEARS

Schroeder found a position as a salesman in a china shop. Next, he served as a commercial apprentice to an ironmonger, until around 1961. That year, he started a job in construction, working on building sites before attending night school and adult education courses. These courses prepared him for his high school graduation certificate, and for Abitur, or A-levels, the certificate of education that qualified him to enter a university.

During these years, there was much happening in his country and abroad. In 1952, West Germany, the United States, France, and Britain signed the Bonn Convention, which gave West Germany almost full national sovereignty. In 1955, the Paris agreements were enforced, granting the nation full independence, although the three former occupying powers continued to maintain troops in West Germany and they reserved the right to negotiate with the Soviet Union on major issues, such as Berlin.

The economy in West Germany grew substantially in the 1950s under the first postwar chancellor, Konrad Adenauer (1876–1967). In 1955, West Germany joined NATO, a military alliance forged in Washington, D.C., in 1949. (Signers of the original document included the United States, Canada, Britain, France, Belgium, Denmark, Iceland, Italy, Luxembourg, Norway, Portugal, and the Netherlands.) In 1958, West Germany also became a charter member of the European Economic Community (EEC, or the Common Market).

The country was also trying to do what it could to atone for

In August 1961, the Soviet Union erected a physical barrier to split East Germany from West Germany, and indeed, East Berlin from West Berlin. The Berlin Wall, seen here being built by East German workers, was a 30-mile-long dividing line that literally and figuratively separated the Communist Soviet Union and its satellite countries from the United States and its allies.

Nazi atrocities. The government paid some reparations to people who were harmed or had suffered losses under the Third Reich. West Germany also contributed significantly to Israel, the Jewish state established in 1948. In 1951, Adenauer signed an agreement pledging more than $800 million in goods to Israel over a 12-year period.

Dramatic events unfolded as the 1960s began. In 1961, East Germany erected a heavily fortified wall that divided East and West Berlin. Its purpose was to prevent East Germans from fleeing the Communist state for democratic West Germany. (Poor working and living conditions and food shortages in East Germany had led to a revolt in 1953, which the Soviet Red Army suppressed.) Although many people were successful in crossing the border (some 4 million passed through between 1945 and 1961), about 200 others were murdered by Soviet troops in the attempt. The Berlin Wall served as a symbolic reminder of the Cold War and the harsh division between the Communist bloc countries and the West.

During this time, Schroeder was becoming engaged in his country's political affairs, learning more and more about the issues that affected him, his fellow Germans, and the world. His family's struggles against poverty surely influenced his early liberal ideas and played a major role in shaping the ideals that informed his politics, particularly his belief in the need for equal opportunities.

When Schroeder was 19 years old, in 1963, he joined West Germany's Social Democratic Party (SPD). The SPD, with leaders such as Kurt Schumacher, Erich Ollenhauer, and Willy Brandt, was the country's primary opposition to the Christian Democratic Union (CDU), Adenauer's more conservative political faction. (In 1949, the CDU, led by Adenauer, formed a coalition with its Bavarian affiliate, the Christian Social Union, or CSU. The CDU-CSU coalition held the majority of seats in the *Bundestag*, the lower house of the German parliament, and helped Adenauer become West Germany's first chancellor.)

Under Adenauer and the CDU-CSU, with help from U.S. President Harry Truman's Marshall Plan, West Germany grew prosperous again. In fact, Germany's remarkable recovery even became known as the "economic miracle." Adenauer strengthened ties with France and successfully established a close alliance with the West. Adenauer was devoted to the reunification of

Germany, but he and his party were initially insistent on doing it according to their own terms. They refused to have diplomatic relations with any country that recognized East Germany. In 1955, however, Adenauer's government initiated formal diplomatic relations with the Soviet Union.

Adenauer retired in 1963, just when Schroeder was developing an interest in politics. Adenauer was replaced by Ludwig Erhard, another Christian Democrat and a noted economist.

It was the Social Democratic Party's more liberal platform, not the policies of the Christian Democrats, that seemed to speak more directly to the 19-year-old Schroeder, who knew firsthand what it meant to be economically disadvantaged. The SPD, which adhered to a pragmatic form of socialism—one promoting social welfare and the interests of workers within a democratic and market-oriented framework—appealed strongly to young Schroeder's ideas about fairness and equality. He grew more active within the party in the mid- to late 1960s, becoming involved in the party's Young Socialists (*Jungsozialisten*, or *Jusos*) movement. He was blossoming into a political activist in the Marxist vein. Most Young Socialists in West Germany at the time embraced Marxism, which is basically the root of all forms of socialism.

By 1964, Schroeder had passed his intermediate high school certificate exam in Goettingen. He continued to work hard and study eagerly, successfully completing his Abitur two years later. Now he was ready for his next step—law school.

3

A Young Activist-Lawyer During the Cold War

When Gerhard Schroeder started law school in 1966, while working part-time to pay for his education, his country was undergoing a tremendous economic surge. Along with rebuilding itself after World War II and creating job opportunities for its citizens, West Germany had also provided shelter and work for nearly 15 million refugees from East Germany and Eastern Europe. West Germany's industry was thriving, running with maximum efficiency and few labor strikes. The refugees supplied cheap and productive labor, and worked hard to start new lives in a democratic state. By the early 1960s, the economy was doing so well that no unemployment problem existed and West Germany had to look to slower-developing nations, such as Italy and Spain, to supply workers. By 1960, West Germany's national income was larger than France's; by 1964, it had overtaken Britain's. The

After World War II, West Germany began a strong friendship with France, despite the fact that they had been bitter enemies during the war. In January 1963, French and German leaders signed a treaty of friendship and agreed to work together toward their mutual goal of integrating Europe. Here, West German Chancellor Konrad Adenauer (left) hugs French President Charles de Gaulle (right) after signing the treaty.

country was, along with France, in a dominant position within the European Economic Community.

Still, the Cold War went on, and West Germany continued to struggle over how to deal with East Germany. Konrad Adenauer's government had maintained that any reunification would be on the West's terms. Adenauer's priorities during the early Cold War years were building capitalism and democracy, and maintaining the alliance with the West—particularly the United States and France. When Ludwig Erhard succeeded Adenauer in 1963, he took a slightly more flexible approach in dealing with East Germany; however, as historian M. Donald

Hancock wrote, Erhard deferred to American leadership on East-West issues: He "stubbornly refused to enter into any sort of dialogue with the East German regime in the absence of a prior American-Soviet agreement on the German question." By 1966, however, a new group was in control of the West German government—the SPD (Schroeder's party) had entered into a coalition government with the CDU. Known as the Grand Coalition, its creation ushered in a new era.

In 1966, West German voters were surprised when Willy Brandt (born Herbert Ernst Karl Frahm; 1913–1992), the SPD chairman who had gained world attention as the mayor of West Berlin, agreed to a temporary partnership with the CDU. When the Christian Democrat candidate, Kurt Georg Kiesinger (1904–1988), was elected chancellor in December, Brandt assumed the posts of vice chancellor and foreign minister.

For the first time since the 1920s, the Social Democrats held some national authority, proving to the CDU and some skeptical West Germans that they were a legitimate, responsible party. Brandt, the son of a young, single shop girl and an activist since his youth, had shown extraordinary courage when the Berlin Wall was erected, and he worked tirelessly for the freedom of West Berlin. Brandt continued to impress West Germany and the world with his skill in economic matters and foreign policy during his tenure as foreign minister. Schroeder, the law student and Young Socialist, watched Brandt's career closely.

In the late 1950s, Brandt had been the main architect of a major revision in the SPD platform. Essentially, the SPD separated itself from its more Marxist past and established a new identity with broader electoral appeal. The party adopted the Bad Godesburg Program, in which it accepted and acknowledged the capitalist system that was already in place, and promoted European integration and cooperation with the West. Although the SPD continued to appeal to its faithful base of industrial workers, it counted middle-class voters among its supporters by the 1960s.

THE STUDENT MOVEMENT

Schroeder started law school at Goettingen University in 1966. During these years of study, he continued to work and also managed to become more involved in leftist politics. He came of age at a heady time for a left-leaning future politician. The late 1960s in Europe were characterized by large-scale and well-organized student protests. In 1966, student associations, trade unions, writers, artists, and others had banded together to create the so-called Extraparliamentary Opposition group. They all agreed that there was no effective parliamentary opposition in West Germany's two-party Grand Coalition and that another voice was needed to represent the people. In June 1967, inspired by student rallies in the United States and the strong global movement against the war in Vietnam, students in West Germany joined together to oppose a visit by the shah of Iran. They also agitated against the traditional administration of German universities, rallied for the abolition of a chain of conservative newspapers, and marched against American involvement in Vietnam. Students staged sit-ins and mass demonstrations during the summer and fall of 1967, and these protest movements culminated in a huge march on Bonn in 1968. Schroeder, who was a mainstream Marxist at that time, participated in some of these protests.

Although many demonstrations were peaceful, a few more radical activists engaged in aggressive tactics to procure their political aims. Besides confrontations with university officials and police forces that turned violent, they also launched attacks on police stations, U.S. military installations, department stores, and other sites that represented capitalism.

THE WILLY BRANDT YEARS

By 1971, Schroeder's involvement with the SPD had so intensified that he became the head of the Young Socialists in Hanover, the state capital of Lower Saxony. By then, Schroeder was married, having wed his childhood sweetheart, librarian

The late 1960s were a time of turmoil and protest not only in Europe but all over the world. In this February 1968 photograph, university students from socialist organizations are protesting the Vietnam War. They are demanding the withdrawal of American troops so that the North Vietnamese can continue to carry out their Communist revolution.

Eva Schubach, in 1968. But he divorced Schubach three years later when his political career began to take off, marrying teacher and political activist Anne Taschenmacher a year after his divorce.

Meanwhile, Willy Brandt, who had become chancellor in 1969, was taking West Germany in a different international direction. Brandt was able to secure the chancellorship after his party formed a new coalition government with the small but influential middle-class-oriented Free Democratic Party

(FDP). For the first time, the Christian Democrats were relegated to the role of opposition party. As Oskar LaFontaine, a future SPD leader, wrote in *The Heart Beats on the Left*:

> In the eyes of us students he [Willy Brandt] quickly became a hero, especially as, in contrast to many other politicians, he had fought in the wartime resistance against the Nazis. . . . His first statement of policy as German chancellor in 1969 had as its motto "Pluck Up Courage for More Democracy." This was a cry that united the hopes of the younger generation. And the coalition of Social Democrats and Free Democrats did indeed succeed in introducing a series of important reforms. Brandt's slogan was no empty promise.

Brandt inspired a generation of left-leaning politicians, including Schroeder.

Domestically, Brandt and his FDP coalition partners put forth a highly ambitious platform for social and economic reform. He successfully fought for the passage of more liberal laws in areas such as abortion and divorce. His government was not able to push much legislation through to overhaul the university system, although Brandt did manage to create new educational opportunities for middle- and working-class children, and establish some new universities. In the international arena, however, Brandt and his government initiated a new era of markedly improved relations between East and West and promoted European unity by encouraging the expansion of the Common Market.

Brandt was the mastermind behind *Ostpolitik* (Eastern policy), a pragmatic foreign policy that emphasized reconciliation with East Germany, other Communist nations in Eastern Europe, and the Soviet Union. He sought to relax tensions with these countries while acknowledging the "territorial integrity" of the respective parties. In 1970, Brandt and Walter Scheel, his minister for foreign affairs, met with Willi Stoph, the East German prime minister, signifying the first time that the top politicians from the two nations had held talks since 1948. Although no solid results came out of the negotiations, the meeting represented an opening up of relations between the two formerly hostile nations. In August 1970, Brandt signed the Treaty of Moscow, a pact of nonaggression and cooperation with the Soviet Union. This agreement led to negotiations with other countries in the Communist bloc. After several months of complicated talks, Brandt went to Poland to sign the Treaty of Warsaw in December 1970, normalizing relations between the two nations. As in the Treaty of Moscow, the countries vowed to "settle all their disputes exclusively by peaceful means."

Brandt's negotiations with the Communist nations caused a great deal of controversy. Although most of West Germany backed Brandt's actions, many conservatives felt that he had conceded too much to the Soviet Union and Poland and compromised West German national interests.

Brandt's efforts led to the signing in September 1971 of the Four Powers agreement. The four former occupying powers vowed to improve access to West Berlin and allow West Berliners to visit East Germany more often. Since 1948, the Soviets and East Germans had blocked Western civilian traffic to and from Berlin.

Brandt and his government also made significant contributions regarding the European Economic Community. Since the early 1960s, Great Britain, Ireland, Denmark, Norway, and Sweden had tried to be admitted to the EEC. The countries—particularly Great Britain—had consistently met with resistance from France, specifically from President Charles de Gaulle. When de Gaulle stepped down in 1969, however, Brandt saw an opportunity to encourage expansion of the EEC. In December 1969, the six EEC countries met, reaffirming their political unity and agreeing to expand the organization. By January 1973, Great Britain, Ireland, and Denmark had signed full EEC membership treaties. (Sweden did not join until 1995, while voters in Norway rejected admission.) Staunchly committed to European unity, Brandt was

West German Chancellor Willy Brandt, who served from 1969 to 1974, worked hard to improve relations between his democratic nation and the surrounding Communist countries. In 1970, Brandt made a visit (seen here) to the Jewish Heroes' Monument in Warsaw, Poland, during a series of meetings with other national leaders.

the leader who most actively promoted the admission of Britain and the other nations to the EEC.

The Bundestag reelected Brandt, who had been awarded a Nobel Peace Prize in December 1971 for his determined efforts to achieve a reconciliation between West Germany and the nations of the Soviet Communist bloc. After his reelection, he continued to press for a comprehensive treaty with the East. In December 1972, East Germany and West Germany signed a Basic Treaty. In it, both sides recognized each other's independence and sovereignty and agreed to work toward improved relations. In 1973, the Bundestag approved the treaty. Not everyone supported the agreement, though. Many conservatives in the CDU-CSU viewed the treaty as a colossal failure, one that symbolized the impossibility of German reunification. As a result of the pact, East and West Germany were admitted to the United Nations in 1973.

Brandt resigned in May 1974, after he discovered that his close assistant, Gunther Guillaume, was a spy for East Germany. Even after he left office, Brandt remained chairman of the SPD until 1987. His vision and actions profoundly influenced Schroeder and a host of other Social Democrats. When Chancellor Schroeder visited Poland before a summit in Nice, France, he said, "Without Willy Brandt and his *Ostpolitik,* without his vision of a free Europe, I would not be standing here."

RADICAL LAWYER

Schroeder successfully passed his first qualifying law examination in 1971. For the next few years, he worked as a lawyer-in-training; in 1976, he passed his second qualifying exam and was admitted to the bar. He was 32. When he opened up his private practice in 1978, he was already an influential young politician in the SPD. His fame grew when he defended Horst Mahler, a founder of the Red Army Faction, a radical, left-wing terrorist organization popularly known as the Baader-Meinhof Gang. The group's declared objective was to overthrow Western capitalism, and its members were self-proclaimed revolutionary Marxists. The group was notorious for its brutality, and after its two leaders (Andreas Baader and Ulrike Meinhof) were imprisoned in 1972, the organization stepped up its campaign. In 1977, it kidnapped the president of the Federation of German Employers' Association. Schroeder defended Mahler at his high-profile parole hearing (1976–1978). The young liberal lawyer with collar-length hair cut quite a figure.

In 1977, Schroeder became a member of the SPD Executive Committee for Hanover, and in 1978, he was elected federal chairman of the Young Socialists. By this time, Schroeder had also organized protests against U.S. policies and against the deployment of NATO missiles in Germany. After it was discovered that the Soviet Union had new intermediate-range missiles and had rapidly increased its nuclear strength, NATO declared that it, too, would introduce new missiles. Speaking when he was chancellor about his earlier politics and Marxist activity, Schroeder said in *Stern* magazine that he was "involved in the planning of the revolution, albeit a social democratic revolution." As his career progressed, he would leave behind the more radical brand of politics that characterized much of his youth.

4

Schroeder Serves His Government

W hen Gerhard Schroeder was 36 years old, in 1980, his political career gained more steam. Representing the SPD from the district of Hanover in Lower Saxony, Schroeder was elected to the Bundestag.

GERMANY'S POLITICAL SYSTEM

Governing responsibilities in Germany are divided between the federal government and the states. The federal government (*Bundesregierung*) handles most significant policy legislation, including matters such as finance, foreign affairs, and defense. The states (*Lander*) deal with the police, cultural affairs, environmental protection, and education. There are 16 states, and each has its own government and legislature. The heads of the states' governments are called minister-presidents (or prime ministers).

The historic Reichstag building (seen here) is the home of the German parliament. Although it had been closed for four years of renovation work, the building reopened for use in April 1999.

As mandated by the Basic Law (Germany's democratic constitution), the federal government is parliamentary in nature. It has a bicameral legislature—the *Bundesrat* (or Federal Council) is the upper house of Parliament, and the *Bundestag* (or National Assembly) is the lower house.

The 69 members of the Bundesrat are appointed by the Lander, and they have no set terms. They are empowered to represent their states' interests on policy issues. All government bills must be submitted first to the Bundesrat for review. The federal president (*Bundesprasident*), who is elected by a federal convention for a five-year term, plays largely a ceremonial role. The president wields limited political power, and is expected to remain nonpartisan while in office. All government bills must be submitted first to the Bundesrat for review.

The Bundestag holds most of the legislative power in the federal government. Members are elected to four-year terms by a popular vote and an electoral system. In order to attain representation in the Bundestag, a party has to obtain a minimum of 5 percent of the national vote or win three seats in the districts. The Bundestag currently has 598 seats. Members of both houses argue policy issues, make laws, and maintain the national budget. The chancellor (*Bundeskanzler*), elected from the Bundestag and usually the head of the party with the most seats in the legislature, exercises executive power. The chancellor cannot be removed from office during his four-year term unless the Bundestag has agreed on a successor. The chancellor appoints a vice chancellor (*Vizekanzler*) who is a member of his cabinet, typically the foreign minister. When there is a coalition government, the minority party in the coalition usually has this slot.

THE POLITICAL CLIMATE SHIFTS

When Gerhard Schroeder delivered his first speech as a member of the Bundestag, he did not wear a tie, insisting that he "wanted to breathe fresh life into Parliament's stodgy ranks." Schroeder's easygoing style and self-deprecating humor made him popular with his constituents and many of his fellow SPD members. One famous anecdote from this period illustrates how ambitious the young politician was.

One night in the early 1980s, he and some friends who were out drinking made their way to the offices of the chancellory in Bonn. (Helmut Kohl was chancellor at the time.) Schroeder climbed the iron gates, rattling them loudly as he yelled, "I want to get in there" until the police arrived and demanded that he get down.

In 1984, Schroeder divorced Anne Taschenmacher and married his third wife, Hiltrud Hampel. A socialite, Hilu (as she was nicknamed) was an animal rights activist and environmentalist. In an attempt to persuade Schroeder to introduce a state law to protect bats, she once brought an injured bat to his office. The couple appeared frequently in gossip columns and became something of a celebrity pair during the 1980s.

While Schroeder served in the Bundestag, another political shift was occurring in West Germany. After Willy Brandt stepped down as chancellor in 1974, he was succeeded by Helmut Schmidt (1918–), his finance minister. When the economy started to deteriorate in the mid- to late 1970s, the SPD-FDP government suffered a considerable loss of popularity. There were also policy disputes within the coalition: Whereas the SPD endorsed higher taxes and increased public borrowing to plump up the economy, the FDP sought to reduce taxes and public services to stimulate recovery. To further complicate the situation, Schmidt's backing of NATO's controversial rearmament created disagreements with the left wing of his own party. When NATO announced that 560 American Pershing II and cruise missiles were to be installed in Western Europe in 1983, large anti-American and antinuclear demonstrations were held throughout West Germany. The coalition's problems were compounded when a new party, the Greens—made up of more liberal deserters from the FDP and SPD, Marxists, and voters concerned with ecological issues—emerged in 1980. The clashes between the SPD and FDP continued to divide the parties until 1982, when the FDP resigned from the cabinet, withdrawing from the coalition.

On October 1, 1982, the CDU-CSU candidate Helmut Kohl (1930–   ), former minister-president of Rhineland-Palatinate, became the new chancellor, signifying a dramatic return to a more conservative government in West Germany. The FDP had joined in a coalition government with the CDU-CSU. Kohl's government endorsed NATO policies and continued to support the presence of NATO forces and American weapons in West Germany. The CDU/CSU-FDP coalition also pursued a conservative approach to economic recovery, emphasizing a gradual reduction in federal spending (and putting Kohl in disfavor with the unions). Kohl's rightist government maintained power in Germany until 1998—the year Schroeder was elected chancellor.

GERMAN REUNIFICATION

After six years in the Bundestag, Schroeder returned to Lower Saxony in 1986. That year, he made a bid to become minister-president of Lower Saxony's state government, but he was unsuccessful, losing to the CDU incumbent, Ernst Albrecht. Next, Schroeder served as opposition leader in the Lower Saxony parliament and headed the SPD group in the parliament until 1990. By this time, historic events had occurred, greatly transforming Germany's European and global role.

During Mikhail Gorbachev's term as leader of the Soviet Union, his radical programs of *glasnost* (openness) and *perestroika* (restructuring) resulted in rampant criticism of the Communist Party. In 1989, political upheavals erupted in Soviet-supported Eastern European nations, and those Communist regimes gradually dissolved. That year, East Germans took to the streets to protest against the Communist regime that ran the nation and its leader, Erich Honecker. Thousands of East Germans fled to West Germany via

Czechoslovakia, Poland, and Hungary. When East Germany closed its borders to halt the exodus, mass demonstrations were staged in every major East German city. Civil unrest spread, and without Soviet support, the regime collapsed. In October, Honecker resigned; in November, the entire council of ministers stepped down, Hans Modrow was elected prime minister, and the *politburo* (the East German legislature) resigned and was reorganized. The new government vowed to initiate political and economic reforms and to hold free elections in 1990. Constraints on the media were partially lifted, a general amnesty was announced for demonstrators who had been arrested and people who had tried to flee the country, and travel restrictions between East and West Germany were abolished. On November 9, the government opened the border between West and East Berlin. Soon, enthusiastic Germans began to physically dismantle the mighty Berlin Wall, so long a symbol of the Cold War.

That month, Chancellor Kohl presented a plan for reunification to the Bundestag, where it was overwhelmingly approved. In the middle of 1990, leaders of East and West Germany, along with the four powers that occupied Germany after World War II, held their "Two-Plus-Four Talks." In May 1990, East and West Germany signed a treaty that established a monetary, economic, and social union, which went into effect on July 1. On October 3, a state treaty formally united them. On December 2, the first all-German elections were held. Kohl, with strong support, was elected chancellor of the reunited nation. In 1991, the Bundestag voted to name Berlin the new capital (but that change did not become official until several years later, when Schroeder was chancellor). The united Germany was also made a full member of NATO. In 1994, the last Allied and Russian troops left Berlin.

After the merriment died down, the Kohl government

In 1990, as Communist nations began to disintegrate after the fall of the Berlin Wall, East and West Germany began the reunification process. Seen here amid the October 1990 celebrations of the reunification, West German Chancellor Helmut Kohl (second from left) shakes hands with East German Premier Lothar de Maiziere.

had to contend with some serious problems. The new united Germany faced escalating unemployment in the eastern part of the country; many eastern businesses suffered against western competition. Kohl increased taxes to support development in the east; he (and Schroeder after him) had the extremely challenging task of trying to transform that part of the nation into a technologically advanced market economy. Also, the east was an environmental mess, with pollution choking urban areas. During all this, the federal deficit rose because of higher welfare and pension costs. Even so, Germany, with its dominant manufacturing sector (especially in the fields of automobiles, chemical products, metals and metal products, and electrical and nonelectrical machinery), was still an economic leader in Europe and the rest of the world—and it was only getting stronger.

MINISTER-PRESIDENT SCHROEDER

Somewhere along the line, during the 1980s, Gerhard Schroeder gave himself a political makeover. As he grew older and more determined in his political ambitions, his far-left tendencies receded and he eventually moved more toward the center. He became a free-market advocate, backing more modern, pro-investment policies. This was a drastic change from his early Marxist roots, and it created tension between him and many traditional Social Democrats. Still, he held onto his belief in social justice and equal opportunity. Somehow he managed to straddle both worlds. As journalist Terence Nelan wrote in 1998, "He is equally at home in one of his trademark Italian suits, smoking cigars with business pals, as he is passionately pleading for a fairer society." He developed a reputation for his pragmatism, and for his ability to build consensus. Schroeder had learned how to use the media to his advantage, and he and his wife, Hilu, became popular in the press, like Bill and Hillary Clinton were in the United States before Clinton's presidency. Schroeder had grown into a savvy politician, and he came across as charming and likable.

Surely these factors helped him become the minister-president of Lower Saxony in 1990. His SPD defeated the CDU to become the strongest party in the state with 44.2 percent of the vote. He formed what became known as the Red-Green coalition, a combination of the SPD and the pro-environment Green Party. His wife's relationship with members of the Green Party helped him. In an article in *Maclean's*, one of Schroeder's associates said that Hilu, an ardent defender of animal rights and the environment, "gave

On February 26, 1990, Lower Saxony's state Prime Minister Gerhard Schroeder (left) joined with German Social Democratic Party leader Oskar LaFontaine (right) at a campaign rally before the March 1 state elections.

him the credibility he needed among the tree huggers and their friends." In his first speech as minister-president, Schroeder announced that his new government would be based on "modernization of the economy, ecological reason, social justice, and cultural variety." However, his "Social-Democratic pragmatism" led him to butt heads often with his Green coalition partners and colleagues in his own party.

During his time as minister-president (he was reelected in 1994 and 1998), he supported more and more programs that strayed from the traditional Social Democratic platform. He pushed for a society that was less dependent on public welfare, and he promoted more labor flexibility and "reasonable wage claims." He endorsed reforms like welfare-to-work programs (as in the United States and Great Britain). Schroeder developed relationships with big businesses, sitting on the board of Volkswagen AG, Lower Saxony's largest employer and a company in which the state had big investments. He also implemented a rigorous budget, which was opposed by many in his party because so many jobs would be lost in the schools and the police force.

Elements of Schroeder's socialist tendencies did show when a struggling Salzgitter steel company underwent a state-sponsored buyout. Schroeder spent $580 million in state money to prevent the company from being sold to an Austrian corporation. He maintained he did it to save more than 12,000 jobs. Schroeder's critics, however, saw the move as evidence that he was beholden to the trade unions; they also thought it telling that it happened just before the Lower Saxony regional elections.

Schroeder's willingness to distance himself from his party on some major policy issues created much tension among the SPD leadership. Still, he seemed to have learned from some of his colleagues' political mistakes. Oskar LaFontaine, the SPD challenger to Chancellor Kohl in 1990, was unashamedly leftist in his agenda, working steadily to support the trade unions, which make up the party's largest constituency. LaFontaine, however, alienated much of the West German electorate when he put workers' rights ahead of the rapid privatization of former East German businesses. Where LaFontaine had stressed the demand side of the issues—increasing jobs and benefits for the workers while cutting taxes—Schroeder was more concerned with the supply side, emphasizing greater flexibility and technological innovation while reducing labor costs.

By the mid-1990s, Schroeder had become a central figure in the SPD and was more immersed in politics at the federal level. After Rudolf Scharping became the SPD chairman in 1993, he named Schroeder a member of his "shadow cabinet," with Schroeder focusing on issues involving energy, economics, and traffic. Scharping, Schroeder, and LaFontaine formed the so-called SPD Troika. They were the most prominent and significant figures in the SPD, considered the successors, or "grandchildren," of Willy Brandt. The three men were very different from one another. Whereas LaFontaine was the hard leftist, Schroeder was a media darling and the star, more popular with the public than with his party colleagues. Scharping, meanwhile, the youngest of the three, was very much a pragmatist, who was more at home with business leaders than with members of the Green Party.

Each man had his own ambitions. When Scharping lost the federal election for the chancellorship in 1994, he became the leader of the SPD parliamentary group in the Bundestag. His colleagues in the party started to question his leadership, though, believing he was stiff, uncharismatic, and not aggressive enough to be chairman. So, in November 1995, with Schroeder's backing, LaFontaine, not Scharping, was elected the new SPD chairman. Scharping did, however, remain parliamentary leader in the Bundestag.

By the time the 1998 election came around, Scharping

was out of the running for the chancellorship. And polls showed that the SPD had a better chance at defeating Kohl and the CDU with Schroeder instead of LaFontaine. When Schroeder won 47.9 percent of the vote in state elections in Lower Saxony in March 1998, LaFontaine threw his full support behind Schroeder, who became the SPD candidate to face Kohl in the federal election.

5

The Campaign for the Chancellorship

When Gerhard Schroeder declared his candidacy for the federal chancellorship in March 1998, German voters had a lot on their minds. The unemployment rate was rising to more than 10 percent; extremely generous social-benefits programs had sent taxes sky-high; the nation was grappling with European integration and a single European currency; and immigration issues had become troublesome. Germans were cautious of change, however. Helmut Kohl had been chancellor for 16 years, had presided over the reunification of East and West, and had forged a stronger alliance with the rest of Europe.

As journalist Dan Williams wrote for CNN before the election, "Germans aren't just electing a chancellor on September 27. They are, arguably, crowning Europe's most powerful man." The nation, with about 82 million people, is Europe's most populous country.

It produces one-tenth of the world's exports and takes in one-twelfth of the world's imports. The chancellor would be at the helm of an economy that is "the engine" of Europe. As Europe was becoming increasingly more integrated and powerful, Germany's new chancellor would play a central role on the international stage.

THE GERMAN CLINTON?

The leadership of the SPD had long recognized Schroeder's charm and telegenic appeal. Next to Kohl, who was 14 years older, the 54-year-old Schroeder appeared energetic and modern. Schroeder and his team were quick to capitalize on Schroeder's charisma and youth. One advertisement shown in German cinemas featured a group of astronauts, with rousing orchestral music playing in the background, being beamed to another planet. The slimmer ones, including Schroeder, made it. The slower, bulkier one, however, was left behind. The message: Filled with youth and vitality, Schroeder was the man who would carry Germany into the future, not the tired and worn-out Helmut Kohl. Many believed that Schroeder could be the face of a new, more modern Germany.

Schroeder became famous for his brief, ten-minute speeches, which contrasted wildly with Kohl's long-winded style. According to reporter Jordan Bonfante in *Time*, Schroeder once said, "People don't want to listen to hour-long oratory anymore." As a media-savvy, left-centrist trying to take over the reins of a country after years of conservative rule, Schroeder was inevitably compared to the U.S. president at the time, Bill Clinton, and to the British prime minister, Tony Blair. (Clinton, a Democrat, began his presidency after 12 years of Republican rule in the White House; Blair's Labour Party took over after 18 years of conservative Tory rule.)

Like Schroeder, Clinton and Blair had liberal roots but

In September 1998, just weeks before the scheduled election for German chancellor, Gerhard Schroeder addressed an SPD rally. Some observers attributed Schroeder's popularity to his fashionable, American-style image, which seemed to many Germans an improvement over the more conservative incumbent Helmut Kohl.

had moved closer to the center, becoming moderates; Clinton and Blair were willing to cross party lines to achieve their goals. Schroeder admired them both. After praising Clinton's trip to China—pointing out his judicious, skillful way of addressing human-rights issues in tandem with his "pragmatic approach" to issues of trade—Schroeder said to a group of U.S. and British journalists: "Americans have an unusually successful president in Bill Clinton." Schroeder and Clinton also shared somewhat similar backgrounds: Both came from very humble, rural beginnings, and had poor-boy-made-good images.

Schroeder even modeled his campaign strategy on Clinton's presidential campaigns, hiring an advisor from Clinton's team. Clinton's 1992 "It's the economy, stupid" slogan inspired Schroeder's catchphrase, "Jobs and the middle class." It was a tactic that would help Schroeder, a politician associated with the left, appeal to the right.

Schroeder has also been criticized for possessing some of Clinton's less appealing traits, though. Like "Slick Willie," as Clinton was sometimes nicknamed, Schroeder, too, was called an opportunist. The CDU leadership and the media labeled him a chameleon: *Die Zeit* magazine declared that Schroeder was "the greatest orator with nothing to say." Commentator Herbert Prantl once told *The New York Times* that Schroeder "is not someone whose heart and soul depend on a particular message. He can change, and one twist suits him as well as the next. What Schroeder likes is whatever is liked by the public he needs at that time." Even Helmut Kohl said that Schroeder was "the most unprincipled challenger I know."

Like Clinton, Schroeder faced a bit of a controversial sex scandal, which brought him some attention he could have done without. The media latched onto the story when they found out that the married Schroeder was seeing another woman, journalist Doris Kopf, in 1996. After his marriage to Hilu Hampel fell apart, Hampel wrote a biting exposé of their relationship. Schroeder and his SPD team were probably concerned that this unwanted attention might cost him some votes from Roman Catholics, who generally condemn extramarital affairs and who make up about 34 percent of Germany's population. After the dirty laundry aired, though, Schroeder's popularity had barely suffered; he was still a public favorite.

Schroeder married the petite, blond Kopf, who is 19 years younger, soon after his divorce. When asked about his divorce from Hampel and marriage to Kopf, Schroeder said, "It's proof of my earnestness." According to *Maclean's*, he remarked: "I'm a constant guy. I may swap wives every 12 years, but I'm faithful in between." Kopf supposedly commented, "Next time, you'll need somebody to push your wheelchair."

THE NEW MIDDLE

The constant comparisons to Clinton and Blair during Schroeder's campaign led many media pundits to place him among a group of leaders representing the so-called Third Way. Like Clinton and Blair, Schroeder is a free-market advocate with close ties to business. Their left-of-center brand of politics rejects traditional socialist policies of big government and big spending but is still concerned with social justice. Blair's sensitive yet practical welfare-to-work programs embodied this ideology, as did Clinton's proposed budget during his second term. Besides Blair and Clinton, social democratic leaders in Northern European countries such as Sweden and the Netherlands had long followed similar compassionate yet pragmatic models.

Although Schroeder did not use the term "Third Way" to describe himself (he has said he is skeptical of using what he considers "philosophical catchwords"), he realized he was part of a growing group of like-minded politicians. "The main question," he said, "is balance. How to modernize the society and modernize the economy, and have social security. How to keep that balance." Schroeder and his team dubbed his political philosophy, "*Die neue Mitte*," or "the new middle." He once said, "There is no longer a conservative or a social democratic

In some ways, Schroeder has modeled his government on the policies of U.S. President Bill Clinton (left) and British Prime Minister Tony Blair (right), who are seen here before the start of the June 1999 G8 summit.

economic policy. There is only the question of old-fashioned or modern economic policy."

During his campaign, Schroeder said that he would reinvigorate Germany's troubled economy, making it more competitive by reducing labor costs. He also said he would lower the unemployment rate and cut back on the mammoth welfare program while not hurting those in real need.

Schroeder's task would be extremely difficult, however. Unlike the United States and Britain, Germany has long had a very generous social welfare system that its citizens, conservatives and liberals alike, have come to take for granted. Although Schroeder praised Blair's welfare-to-work program, a Schroeder aide acknowledged that the German candidate would have a far greater challenge than his British counterpart: "Blair himself would not be Blair without the [Prime Minister Margaret] Thatcher reformation that came before him. Blair's been handed a deregulated economy on a golden platter. Germany has not undergone that reformation."

But Schroeder also claimed to be committed to maintaining Germany's strong social benefits package. In speeches along the campaign trail, he spoke about how cutting benefits would hurt widows like his mother. He promised that if elected, he would roll back a few of the reforms Kohl had pushed through, such as reducing sick pay for some workers from full pay to 80 percent, and lowering corporate pension contributions. Schroeder said, "Especially burdened by these reductions is the generation of elderly women who lost their husbands in the war and were never afforded the luxury of a second income while they helped rebuild Germany and raised children on their own." He added, "I consider it rude for a country as rich as Germany to reduce pensions for this part of society."

Schroeder's number-one priority was his "Alliance for Jobs" initiative, a program that would include round-table discussions among employers, unions, and government officials. His government would make a deep investment to ease unemployment, focusing on training programs for young people. Yet it would also curtail overtime. (The overall German unemployment rate was around 11 percent during the campaign; but in the region of the former East Germany it was about double that number.) As to how Schroeder would manage to roll back the Kohl reductions while putting so much into the creation of new jobs, Schroeder described a broad tax reform plan that would create savings. This proposal created a stir within his party—an increase of taxes was not something that sat well with many Social Democrats. "Schroeder [was] trying to open up new ways for two important things: employment and entrepreneurship," said Bela Anda, editor of *Bild-Zeitung* and Schroeder's biographer. "The things he will have to do could be quite harsh, but no one is in a better position to deliver this bitter pill than he is." Schroeder's approach was also geared to appeal to the many young voters who, concerned with the growing unemployment rate, were ready for a change. "The new middle appeals to all those who want to grasp the initiative in their jobs and training, experience the growing flexibility of the labor market. The new middle appeals to those who want to fulfill the dream of self-employment, who are willing to take risks," Schroeder said.

Schroeder's detractors singled out the high unemployment rate and rapidly rising deficit in Lower Saxony as proof of his failure in his state. Schroeder responded that he had actually saved jobs and kept unemployment around the same rate. He once said, according to journalist Mary Williams Walsh in *The New York Times*, "It's always better to invest in jobs than to invest in unemployment."

Germany's social-benefits program had stretched the federal budget virtually to the breaking point, though. The cost of hiring workers in Germany is among the highest in the world. Welfare and unemployment benefits are so lavish that many people would prefer to lose a job than to have one. Schroeder, however, was presenting no solution radical enough to turn things around. Nor, for that matter, was Kohl. In fact, it seemed to many that Schroeder and the SPD ultimately backed many of the same tax reforms that Kohl and the CDU did.

In the final days leading up to the September 1998 election, Gerhard Schroeder addressed this large campaign meeting (he is seen on the giant TV screen), in hopes of winning any remaining undecided votes.

Schroeder felt that many Germans were wary of change and needed reassurance instead of drastic measures. "You can only take people with you on a journey to change if you give them the most basic measure of security," he commented. One of Schroeder's slogans spoke directly to allaying that fear of change: "We won't change everything—we'll just do things better."

Schroeder's critics said that underneath his charm and energy was a steady stream of contradictions: He was close to industry leaders, who gave him the nickname "comrade of the bosses." He pledged modernization and innovation so Germany would maintain its economic strength, but promised to continue supporting workers and social programs. Schroeder stood by his pragmatic approach, saying, "I am neither right nor left. I am a human being."

His critics also cited his evasiveness when it came to certain issues, such as Germany's role in the European Community. He seemed to lack solutions for economic revitalization in the former East Germany. He also equivocated about whether he favored a single European currency. In March 1998, he said that the euro (the common currency used by European Union countries) was "a sickly premature infant," the result of an "overhasty monetary union." Then he changed his tune. Schroeder ultimately vowed that he would continue along the same path paved by Kohl in regard to the euro and European integration. (Kohl had pushed hard for the euro, even though many Germans feared giving up their beloved deutsche mark, a symbol of their postwar economic success.)

In fact, Schroeder promised to maintain most of Kohl's foreign policy practices, including his approach toward the United States and NATO. Indeed, after all the rhetoric and campaign strategies, Schroeder and Kohl seemed to have similar goals and political values. Two weeks before the election, about 40 percent of voters were still undecided. One poll revealed that 73 percent of the undecided voters felt they knew too little about the candidates' platforms or saw too little difference between them.

Even Schroeder struggled to describe how he would be different from Kohl as he led Germany. He said, "Since economic policy has a lot to do with psychology, positive change can only be achieved with a new beginning. That means a new government."

COALITIONS AND PARTY POLITICS

Regardless of how Germans felt about Schroeder's character or campaign platform, voters had ample reason to be concerned about his ability to push programs through the legislature. The SPD, at heart, was still a traditionally leftist party. Although it has a host of self-proclaimed pragmatists within its ranks, it also has many unreconstructed socialist-minded politicians—like Oskar LaFontaine, the SPD chairman. Remaining largely behind the scenes during the 1998 campaign, LaFontaine clearly continued to hold a prominent role in forming SPD policy. He was seen as the mastermind behind the decision to campaign against a tired and worn-out incumbent instead of against a problematic platform. "The people just don't want him anymore," LaFontaine said of Kohl. More moderate or conservative voters were concerned that once Schroeder was elected, his tax-and-spend peers would hold more sway. The German Lander parties, in particular, would present a problem; they are notoriously autonomous and would have difficulty giving up their power. It appeared highly likely that Schroeder would spend much time at loggerheads with elements of his own party. Coalition politics, too, were a cause for concern. Schroeder's ability to effect change would depend in large part on which parties made up the ruling coalition. Germans cast their vote for a party rather than a candidate; then parties negotiate a coalition to create a majority. A chancellor may be named only with a majority. Therefore, votes for the smaller parties determine what type of coalition will be formed.

During the campaign, Schroeder and LaFontaine met with Joschka Fischer, the Green Party parliamentary leader. Although a Red-Green coalition was Schroeder's stated preference, moderates feared that this combination might strengthen the leftists in the SPD and prevent Schroeder from accomplishing his free-market-oriented goals. Others felt that if the race were close, Schroeder would not have a problem with a CDU-SPD Grand Coalition, which might help him implement many of his Third Way–style, pragmatic reforms.

6

A Troubled Start in Office

Voter turnout was very high—61 percent—for the federal Bundestag elections on September 27, 1998. The SPD received the largest share of the vote (about 41 percent), while the CDU won just about 35 percent of the Bundestag seats, its worst results in 40 years. Since the SPD did not gain enough votes to constitute a majority, Gerhard Schroeder and the SPD entered into a coalition government with the Green Party. A month later, Schroeder was elected chancellor of the Federal Republic of Germany, ending 16 years of conservative rule and becoming the first opposition leader in postwar German history to oust an incumbent chancellor.

After the polls closed, Schroeder spoke at his party's head-quarters. He said, "After 16 years, the Kohl era is at an end." He said he would work for "economic stability and development,

Speaker of the Parliament Wolfgang Thierse (right) looked on as newly elected Chancellor Gerhard Schroeder took his oath of office on October 27, 1998.

domestic security, and continuity in foreign affairs." Schroeder promised an end to 16 years of conservative "stagnation," claiming it was his duty to unite and modernize Germany. He also declared, "Dear friends, my most important goal is the struggle against the scourge of mass unemployment." At one point, Schroeder said that his government would not deserve to remain in power if the unemployment rate did not improve. It was a pledge that would come back to haunt him.

During Schroeder's first term, he had to try to tackle the unemployment problem (particularly in the east) and reinvigorate the economy; participate in the establishment of a single European currency and the integration of Europe while maintaining a strong relationship with France; support economic development in Russia; establish a policy on immigration; and maintain a positive relationship with NATO and the United States. He also had to preside over the transfer of the nation's capital from Bonn to Berlin.

Though a number of Germans were optimistic about the change at the federal level, many were skeptical of Schroeder's ability to lead. Would he deliver on his many, and often contradictory, promises? Was he capable of bringing about actual policy changes? How would Schroeder, a man with limited experience in international affairs, handle himself on the global stage? Germans, and the rest of the world, were watching.

RED-GREEN COALITION

To get the majority needed to name a chancellor, the SPD had to enter into a ruling coalition. Although Schroeder would have welcomed a coalition with the CDU (it would have helped him initiate free-market reforms), Kohl rejected it because too much would be sacrificed. So a Red-Green coalition it was. Since the Greens were a broad mix of pragmatists and radicals, however, it was sure to be a rocky relationship. Many were adamant in their stance on controversial issues such as nuclear power and NATO expansion. Schroeder and other pragmatists were concerned that the more extreme elements would impede the march toward economic rejuvenation. Oskar LaFontaine, though, the man largely responsible for drafting the coalition agreement with the Greens, said, "I would be able to carry through a socio-ecological reform program in energy policy and transport policy, and above all promote the cause of world peace." LaFontaine's wish was that the Greens would help Germany avoid military involvement with NATO and phase out its nuclear power program.

Before taking office, Schroeder (at right, behind microphones) answered questions from the media at the side of Green Party leader Joschka Fischer (left of Schroeder). The new government of which Schroeder had recently been elected chancellor would be a coalition of Schroeder's SPD and the Green Party, a so-called Red-Green coalition.

Schroeder named Joschka Fischer, a popular leader of the pragmatic segment of the Green Party, as vice chancellor and foreign minister. The Greens insisted that their environmental agenda become part of the coalition platform and that the coalition adhere to the pledge to gradually abandon the nuclear power program.

CLASHES WITHIN

As several pundits predicted, clashes arose from the start between the camps of the Third Way–driven Schroeder and the traditional socialist LaFontaine, who had been named finance minister. The SPD lacked solidarity, and there was mounting tension and constant infighting among its ranks. LaFontaine, still the SPD leader, wielded considerable power, persuading Schroeder to invest more authority in the finance ministry and less in the economics ministry. (Jost Stollman, a computer magnate and free-market advocate who had been Schroeder's choice to lead the economics ministry, removed himself from consideration upon hearing this news.) LaFontaine's economics did not mesh with Schroeder's supply-side approach. In the first months of SPD rule, LaFontaine, supporting the rights of the worker, shifted the tax burden from households to businesses and the wealthy (without loosening labor regulations). Naturally, he fell in disfavor with big business but pleased the unions. "Red Oskar," as he was called in the media, also proposed an increase in the "value added tax" on goods and services. Furthermore, LaFontaine's calls for reducing interest rates incensed bankers, and his plea for tax harmonization in the European Union irritated Germany's EU partners. The pragmatists and conservatives worried that Schroeder was not strong enough to stick to his goals of modernization and market-oriented reform. After all the campaign talk about reform, Schroeder and LaFontaine scrapped Kohl's cuts in pensions and sick leave, thereby bolstering the welfare state.

Also, the coalition government was moving toward the decommissioning of Germany's nuclear power plants. There were problems, however, that stemmed from the clashing interests of the pragmatics in both the SPD and the Green Party and the more extreme Greens. After the government decided to close the nation's 19 atomic power plants, Jurgen Tritten—the Green Party environmental minister and the head of the party's hard-line wing—announced in February 1999 that all nuclear waste shipments to plants in France and Britain (for reprocessing) would be suspended by the following January. There would be no compensation for severing the million-dollar contracts, though. The French and British governments balked, and German energy companies put an increasing amount of pressure on Schroeder, who postponed the phase-out. This controversy and German anger at the Greens cost Schroeder a majority in the Bundesrat— the Red-Green coalition lost five seats in state elections in Hesse largely because of the nuclear phase-out issue, although voters were also bitter about increased energy taxes and gasoline prices.

Schroeder was not off to a good start. On top of the public bickering, the economy was slowing, unemployment continued to rise, and business confidence was low. In response to LaFontaine's business tax, several companies threatened to close down or leave Germany less than a year into Schroeder's chancellorship. Allianz (a major insurance company) and several other corporations claimed that they would move their operations out of the country. In March 1999, a group of nuclear power industry employers met with Schroeder, demanding that the coalition government reverse its policy. The coalition was in a crisis.

LAFONTAINE RESIGNS

The day after the meeting with the power industry employers, a cabinet meeting grew heated, leading some to believe that Schroeder himself might resign. However, it was LaFontaine who stepped down, immediately retreating to his home in Saarbrucken without discussing his decision with his SPD colleagues. He also gave up the leadership of the SPD. Business chiefs were, not surprisingly, jubilant; they urged Schroeder to scrap the tax reforms just passed by the Bundestag. (Despite their request, the chancellor continued to push them through—

the unions were still a formidable force.) Klaus Zwickel, the head of IG Metall, the nation's largest trade union, criticized LaFontaine for running away and said that his departure was a "first victory for capital." The suddenness of the move caused many to speculate if the coalition government would last. It was LaFontaine, after all, who had orchestrated the agreement with the Greens.

Schroeder immediately did what he could to show that his government was holding together. He named himself SPD chairman and Hans Eichel the finance minister. Still, the SPD was bitterly divided, with almost one-third of the executive refusing to support his leadership at a special party congress in April, when he was officially elected party chairman. The left-leaning wing was concerned that the SPD goals of social justice would suffer in favor of the more moderate goals of modernization and flexibility. It felt that Schroeder would not be strong enough to stand up to big business. The unemployment rate was soaring, and many were concerned that unhappy SPD members would join the PDS (Party of Democratic Socialism), the former Communists. The pragmatic and driven Joschka Fischer and his party announced that they were still devoted to the coalition, but the Greens continued to be split about policy issues.

Judging from the reactions of the markets—the struggling euro rose, and German stock prices shot up—many free-market-minded people had a renewed sense of hope with LaFontaine out of the picture. They anticipated a shift away from tax-and-spend policies and regulation and a move toward opening up the markets. "Red Oskar," the man they saw as the nemesis of progress, was gone.

Remarkably, amid all the chaos, polls revealed that Schroeder's popularity had barely suffered. His party as a whole, however, did face problems. After LaFontaine's departure, the SPD lost several state elections, including crucial ones in Brandenburg and Saarland, and the CDU was regaining some favor. CDU scandals, however, seemed perfectly timed to help boost the SPD's approval ratings. In late 1999, it was discovered that former Chancellor Helmut Kohl and his party had accepted millions of dollars in illegal donations through the 1980s and 1990s.

7

Chancellor Schroeder and Domestic Issues

With the departure of Oskar LaFontaine, Germans watched closely to see if Gerhard Schroeder could redeem himself and save his chancellorship. Free-market proponents and businesses thought that Schroeder would be freed to advance his progressive Third Way goals, now that the trade unions had lost their biggest advocate, LaFontaine. Working-class Germans wondered if they would be left out in the cold, and the new middle class, to which Schroeder appealed during his campaign, was getting impatient and wanted to see some progress. As reflected in the poor performance of the SPD in several state elections, the public was clearly unhappy with his administration. Schroeder needed to assert his leadership.

Although Schroeder's chancellorship was hampered by infighting within the Red-Green coalition, and he continued to be criticized for trying to be all things to all people, Schroeder did eventually achieve

Much of Schroeder's popular support came from the middle class, a relatively new social group to which the stylish and energetic leader appealed.

some of his goals: He passed a hugely ambitious tax-reform bill (the largest in the history of the Federal Republic), initiated a groundbreaking private pension program, implemented a new immigration policy, and eventually came up with a plan to phase out nuclear power. He did not come close to fulfilling his most ardent promise, however. At the end of his term, the unemployment rate in Germany was still extremely high.

TAX REFORM

Schroeder scored a tremendous success in July 2000, when he managed to push through the most extensive tax-reform package in German history. The CDU-controlled Bundesrat passed the Future Program 2000, a multiyear financial plan that was favored by many different interests—including big business, trade unions, and foreign investors. The package, proposed by Finance Minister Hans Eichel and intended to substantially reduce government debt, included significant reductions in state spending as well as tax cuts. Eichel said that it "will bring tax relief amounting to 62.5 billion marks." The victory was a huge one for Schroeder and represented the first urgently needed step toward economic reform and modernization.

As Eichel described, "Families, workers, as well as the small business sector will benefit most from [the tax reform package]. Around 33 billion marks in tax relief will go to private households, and more than 23 billion marks to small and medium-sized companies." By Eichel's estimates, the basic income tax rate would be cut to 15 percent and the top rate to 42 percent by 2005. The corporation tax would decrease from 45 percent to 25 percent, which would hopefully bring more jobs by making Germany more competitive internationally and more attractive to foreign investors. Small- and medium-sized businesses would see a significant reduction in income taxes. Families would reap some rewards, too, receiving more benefits for their first and second children. Also, several tax loopholes beneficial to only the highest wage-earners were closed. Eichel believed that the money freed up for German consumers could go toward more consumption and investment, further bolstering the economy. It was the coalition's hope that by 2005, the government would not have to borrow from foreign nations or businesses anymore. Eichel described the 2000 tax reform package as the "feat of the century." Norbert Walter, chief economist at Deutsche Bank, believed that the program would promote growth. "The tax reform sends an important signal to investors," he said.

Although the packages were almost universally praised, they had their detractors, primarily leftists in Schroeder's ruling coalition. These critics felt that some of the cuts were too harsh on the working and middle classes. Also, the unemployment rate was still hovering around 10 percent by the end

Schroeder's government faced criticism for its inability to heal the ailing economy despite a wide-ranging program of budget cuts and tax reforms. In this 1999 photograph, Schroeder (rear) watches as Finance Minister Hans Eichel takes part in a debate over some controversial budget cuts.

of 2002. It remains to be seen whether Schroeder's attempts at economic reform will succeed in the long term.

PENSIONS

Another focus of the Schroeder administration concerned pensions. With a large segment of German society growing older, pension insurance funds were in danger of being depleted. Schroeder's team acknowledged that the pay-as-you-go state system, in which contributions from those who are currently working are used to support retirees, would no longer be sustainable. So Schroeder proposed that Germans consider investing in private pension funds. The federal employment minister, Walter Riester, planned to make available 20 billion deutsche marks to help the Germans jumpstart their savings. Under Riester's proposal, young employees would start saving 0.5 percent of gross wages in private insurance and pension funds, but would continue to contribute to the state pension system (which is split equally between employers and employees). Schroeder was determined to see this bill passed, saying, "The private pension plan must be pushed through. Otherwise I am afraid the window will be closed forever." After some skillful political maneuvering, Schroeder successfully urged members of the CDU to support his groundbreaking bill, which the Bundesrat passed on May 11, 2001. The state subsidization system (the so-called Riester pension program) went into effect in January 2002.

IMMIGRATION

One of the hot-button issues of Schroeder's election campaign concerned the treatment of immigrants and war refugees. People from Central Europe, Turkey, and the Balkans were flooding into Germany, taking advantage of the political asylum guaranteed in Germany's constitution. Meanwhile, there was a resurgence of racism—skinheads were attacking immigrants and torching the homes of refugees. During his campaign, Schroeder had vowed that his government "will make it possible to have dual citizenship," where immigrants could become German citizens and still retain citizenship in their native countries. When he became chancellor, Schroeder took steps to follow through on his promise, and he received solid backing from the Greens. In 1999, his administration presented a plan to permit people who have lived in Germany for eight years or more to apply for citizenship.

Immigration has long been an issue that raised heated debate in Germany. Under Schroeder's leadership, the German government took steps to change immigration laws to make it easier for newcomers, like this woman who holds both German and Cuban passports, to become citizens.

Before this, the law (which had been in existence since before World War I) said that citizenship was only open to people whose parents were German-born. Schroeder's bill would grant citizenship to anyone born on German soil and allow them to maintain their foreign passports as well.

The bill as Schroeder conceived it was never passed, however. Edmund Stoiber, the archconservative leader of the Christian Social Union (CSU), and Wolfgang Schauble, the CDU leader, led an enormous campaign against the immigration reform, claiming to have collected more than one million signatures. Although the official argument of the CDU-CSU was that dual citizenship would impede the integration of foreigners into German society, many people believed their opposition had an underlying racist agenda. Ultimately, though, a variation of Schroeder's proposal did pass. The issue of dual citizenship was abandoned, but the new law made it easier for 4 million foreigners, mostly Turks, to be naturalized.

In December 2000, the government also lifted a 1997 ban that prevented immigrants and refugees from being employed in Germany. This measure enabled immigrants to work after a period of 12 months, although refugees with permits would be allowed to work immediately. A few days later, Interior Minister Otto Schily announced a new program to help immigrants become part of German society. The $280 million annual program would include vouchers and tuition to help them learn the language and become integrated in other ways.

In August 2000, the government implemented a "green card" program. Schily had previously said that Germany should update its immigration laws to create a more flexible system that would reflect its own economic interests but was "in line with our own political, economic, cultural and demographic interests." The green card system came about in response to the German demand for technology experts in the electronics industry, which needed mathematicians and other highly qualified professionals to stay internationally competitive. (A green card permits immigrants to live and work temporarily in Germany for five years before they would have to return home.) Also, the population growth in Germany, as in many other European nations, is slowing. Projections indicate that without a rise in immigration, Germany's population would decline to 60 million by 2050 from around

82 million today, if there is no increase in immigration. This means that the workforce may shrink to 26 million from 42 million.

Schily proposed the "Law on the restriction and the control of immigration in Germany," which aimed to address the negative and positive effects of immigration. Between 1985 and 1999, about 10.5 million foreigners had entered Germany; the nation received 95,300 applications for political asylum in 1999. Schily said, "We have perhaps occasionally reached the quantitative boundaries on uncontrolled immigration. . . . Immigration can be burdensome, especially when it runs uncontrolled. Open discussion about the issue must be allowed. . . . The positive effects of immigration must be stressed." Germany's immigration policy, according to the commission appointed by Schily, "needs to take account of humanitarian considerations, the country's economic well-being and the integration of immigrants within German society." The commission proposed a controversial point system in which people were assessed according to their academic credentials, fluency in German, and other criteria.

The government presented the bill in 2002, and the Bundesrat effectively passed it. It had to be resubmitted in early 2003, however, due to a minor technical error.

THE NUCLEAR PHASE-OUT AND THE ECO-TAX

In June 2000, the coalition government and nuclear power companies finally came to an agreement to phase out nuclear power within 25 years. The phase-out had been a priority on the Green and SPD agenda during the campaign for the chancellorship, but the parties had difficulty reaching a consensus with the utility companies about how and when the nuclear plants would cease operations. In February 1999, Jurgen Tritten, the environmental minister and Green Party hardliner, declared that contracts with the French and British companies that handled the reprocessing of Germany's nuclear waste would be severed by the following January, and the companies

In June 2000, German government and business representatives came to an agreement in which they decided to gradually shut down Germany's 19 nuclear power stations. This made Germany the first leading nation to abandon the use of nuclear energy.

would not be reimbursed for the loss of millions of dollars in business. The French and British companies, along with the utilities, were furious, and Schroeder felt compelled to postpone the phase-out until a compromise could be reached. Although popular opinion polls revealed that more than 75 percent of Germans wanted an end to the nuclear power program, the powerful utility companies felt that an immediate phase-out was unfair and not economically viable.

After months of negotiations, the administration and the energy industry announced a plan to shut down the country's 19 nuclear power plants over the next three decades. The compromise was praised by the utility companies and criticized by antinuclear activists and leftists in the SPD and Green Party. Under the agreement, the companies would halt operations of their plants after they had operated at full power for approximately

32 years. Energy companies could build no new plants, and after 2005, nuclear waste reprocessing would be banned. The government and the energy industry both avowed their commitment to developing an environmentally sound yet internationally competitive energy program. Of the agreement, Schroeder said, "We have reached a fair compromise. The issue of nuclear energy has been a divisive one in the country. We have found a consensus with the energy industry to get rid of it over the long term." Many Greens, however, felt that the agreement was too much of a compromise, and that Schroeder and Tritten sacrificed too much.

In Schroeder's first term, the Red-Green coalition instituted an eco-tax. The purpose of this Green-developed tax was to discourage energy consumption and encourage conservation by making carbon fuels more costly. There would be a new tax on electricity and an increase in the petroleum tax. The money raised from the program would help the government with pension contributions. Although the tax is deeply unpopular, Finance Minister Hans Eichel said that the eco-tax reform "pursues an important goal in the fight against unemployment: we are using all such revenues to reduce the cost of labor." The coalition partners believed that the tax would promote the use and development of renewable energies. Eichel said,

> Reputable studies have proven that the ecological tax reform is giving significant impetus to a very important growth market: to the development of energy-saving technologies and production processes. . . . Studies demonstrate that more than 200,000 new jobs have been created as a result of the ecological tax reform.

SAME-SEX PARTNERSHIPS

Schroeder's government has also tackled some highly controversial social issues. In December 2000, the German Bundesrat passed a law that extended some legal recognition to gay and lesbian couples. The Red-Green coalition had tried to win ratification for similar legislation previously, but was unable to get it passed by the CDU-CSU-dominated Bundesrat. Progress was made when the Schroeder administration strategically divided the Green-backed bill into two parts—one that the Bundesrat approved and one that it did not.

One part had been passed relatively easily by the coalition-controlled Bundestag in November, and was ratified by the Bundesrat in December. Under this law, which went into effect on August 1, 2001, same-sex couples would be legally permitted to take the same surname, share household insurance, and act as next of kin in significant medical matters. They would also enjoy the same inheritance rights as heterosexual couples. Also, a foreign-born gay or lesbian person in a partnership with a German would earn the right to German citizenship. Legalized gay partnerships, however, also brought more responsibilities to those involved—a partner would now be required to support the other if he or she had financial problems. Another part of the bill, which covered rights in tax and welfare matters, was not approved by the Bundesrat.

Members of the conservative CSU adamantly opposed the new policies, calling them "the greatest attack on the institution of marriage in decades." In July 2001, the states of Bavaria and Saxony lost their battle to ban the law. They had argued that the law violated previous German legislation protecting marriage and the family, but the Federal Constitutional Court rejected their claim. The Green Party declared, "The registration of same-sex partnerships does not damage the family or marriage. The protection of marriage and family life should not mean discriminating against homosexuals."

COMPENSATION

Schroeder also had to deal with problems left over from as far back as World War II. In recent years, several class-action lawsuits had been filed in the United States to recover damages sustained by victims of Nazi-enforced slave labor during the war. During Helmut Kohl's term of office, he maintained that the German companies that used slave laborers should not have to pay the victims, since they were merely following Nazi government orders.

After year-long talks, however, Schroeder's administration hammered out an agreement with representatives of the United States, Israel, Belarus, the Czech Republic, Poland, Russia, and Ukraine, along with the legal representatives of the victims and the German companies. Under the plan, the German government and the industries would finance a special fund to compensate the survivors. In July 2000, Germany's lower house of parliament passed a bill establishing the "Memory, Responsibility, and Future" Foundation. The organization would pay about $7.5 billion to the Jews, Roma (gypsies), and others who were subjected to forced labor during the Nazi era. Of the foundation, Schroeder said, "This closes one of the last open chapters of the Nazi past. We are setting down a durable marker of historical and moral responsibility."

Schroeder said the creation of the foundation was a "long overdue humanitarian gesture." Estimates put the number of slave laborers during the Third Reich at between 6 million and 12 million. The 1.5 million victims still alive today would receive payments of between $2,400 and $7,200, depending on whether they worked in concentration camps (where the conditions were worst of all) or in factories. The legislation would automatically grant the companies immunity from further class-action lawsuits filed by slave-labor victims.

8

Chancellor Schroeder and International Affairs

Before Gerhard Schroeder became chancellor, he had limited experience in international affairs. To make his job even more challenging, he had to follow in the footsteps of Helmut Kohl, who was highly respected in the international community for his great success in overseeing the unification of East and West Germany. Kohl had also enjoyed a solid relationship with the United States, and he ensured that Germany's relationship with France held strong. His administration was a tough act to follow.

During Schroeder's first months in office, he was largely preoccupied with tackling domestic issues—especially the dreadful state of the economy and high unemployment—and he was also

In 1999, Germany was preparing to join NATO and to send some of its own forces to take part in the international peacekeeping mission in Kosovo. As part of those preparations, Chancellor Schroeder (second from left) accompanied Defense Minister Rudolf Scharping (at left) on an inspection of German military recruits.

consumed by the conflicts in his ruling coalition. After all, he had declared that he would put national interests first. However, Schroeder quickly found his diplomatic skills put to the test.

KOSOVO AND NATO

On March 24, 1999, NATO sent an international force to the former Yugoslavia to try to put an end to former Yugoslavian President Slobodan Milosevic's slaughter of ethnic Albanians in Kosovo. Under Milosevic's rule, Serb troops had begun murdering Albanian Kosovars (or forcing them to leave their homes and flee the country) after a movement for an independent Kosovo (free from Serbian rule) had gained momentum. NATO initially responded to the crisis by drawing up a proposal granting Kosovo considerable autonomy, but Milosevic rejected it and even stepped up his ethnic cleansing campaign. Despite repeated warnings from NATO, Serb forces continued the genocide.

The German constitution bans the deployment of troops unless it is part of a NATO action, but Germans had made previous amendments to accommodate the commitment of troops to peacekeeping missions in Somalia and the Balkans. For the first time since World War II, the German government decided to send some of its troops to participate in NATO combat operations. Schroeder also agreed to take in 40,000 Kosovar refugees, more than any other country accepted.

NATO's air campaign focused initially on military sites but gradually expanded its targets to include some of Kosovo's infrastructure. The decision to send combat forces was part of Schroeder's plan for continuity in foreign affairs, and polls showed that more than 60 percent of Germans backed the deployment at the beginning of the campaign. Even Joschka Fischer, a member of the officially pacifist Green Party, supported the move. Many Green hardliners and members of the SPD, however, stridently opposed German military involvement. On Easter Sunday, 1999, 50,000 demonstrators marched in protest against the bombing, and some antiwar activists broke into Green offices and spray-painted "Green warmongers" on the walls. Many Greens demanded that Fischer step down. Gernot Erler, the SPD deputy parliamentary leader, said that the link between the bombing and ending Serbia's atrocities must be "made clearer in the next few days or it won't just be a problem of the SPD but a total breakdown of the consensus of public opinion." And according to *Bild,* Environment Minister Jurgen Tritten said, "For me it is not right that NATO planes should drop splinter bombs and attack civilian targets, such as power plants and television stations. That has got to stop." Again, the Red-Green coalition was openly at odds.

While British Prime Minister Tony Blair pushed for a ground war, believing that the air campaign would not succeed, Fischer backed a peace proposal that ultimately went to NATO—endorsing a 24-hour pause in the bombing campaign to permit Serb forces to pull out of Kosovo. In June, though, Milosevic, somewhat surprisingly, conceded defeat. He signed an agreement that resulted in the end of the bombing campaign, the withdrawal of Serb forces, and the entrance of NATO peacekeeping troops.

AGENDA 2000 AND EUROPEAN INTEGRATION

One of Schroeder's major responsibilities as new chancellor was shepherding Germany through European integration. Schroeder—who held the EU presidency for the first six months of 1999—was committed to enlisting support for his Agenda 2000, a series of reforms that would determine the EU's budgetary structure for the next six years (smoothing the way for the entry of new member states, starting in 2002).

Germany accounts for a large part—around 24 percent—of the European Union's Gross Domestic Product (GDP). Although Schroeder was a strong believer in European unification, he announced that Germany was no longer willing (or able) to contribute as much toward the EU's budget as it had in the past. This stance was a drastic departure, and seemed like something of a breakthrough for Germany's role in Europe. As journalist Roger Cohen wrote in *The New York Times* in 1998, Schroeder had adopted "an almost Thatcherite tone as he lambasted the European Union for draining Germany's resources." The chancellor pointed out that the German net contribution was four times more than that of any other country in the union, and that the reunification of Germany had cost the government billions of dollars. Schroeder said in a speech, "We cannot and do not want to continue a policy that buys the goodwill of our neighbors with net payments that will become a burden to our country. . . . We cannot solve Europe's problems with the German checkbook."

As part of his Agenda 2000, the chancellor pressed for a more equitable distribution of payments among members. The package included deep cuts in the Common Agricultural Policy. This would mostly affect France, which profits most from the agricultural assistance. A special British rebate, however, which had been in place since Margaret Thatcher implemented it in the 1980s, might also be ditched. Schroeder warned that if these measures were not taken to alleviate Germany's financial burden, the EU would not be able to grow.

By April 5, 1999, an agreement had been reached on Agenda 2000. Although it fell short on most of the reforms initially proposed, all of the EU leaders came out of the meetings with "something they could sell back home as success," according to *Time* writer James Graff. Great Britain was able to hold on to its rebate; there were some modifications in the policy to ease the burden on Germany, the Netherlands, Sweden, and Austria; also, while the French did have to make higher payments than in the past, they were able to avoid the deep cuts of the initial proposal. Schroeder praised the meeting as "an extraordinarily successful summit." Prime Minister Blair described Schroeder's achievements at guiding the 15 states toward unity as "brilliant chairmanship."

A STRAINED ALLIANCE WITH FRANCE

In late 1999, Schroeder and Blair released a historic document, *Europe: The Third Way—Die Neue Mitte*, which called for welfare reform, flexible labor markets, and corporate tax cuts. The French prime minister, Lionel Jospin, immediately distanced himself from it. Jospin, a traditional socialist, felt that the proposal was anti–working class, and did not regulate business strongly enough. He did not agree with Schroeder and Blair's promotion of "flexible" labor markets at the expense of workers' rights. Jospin was also concerned about something else—for years, France and Germany had enjoyed a strong alliance. Now that the German capital had moved from Bonn to Berlin, there was concern that the relationship would be weakened

In March 1999, the foreign ministers who act as European Union representatives met to discuss several issues, including the situation in Kosovo. Here, French Foreign Minister Hubert Vedrine (left) and German Foreign Minister Joschka Fischer (center) listen to their British colleague, Robin Cook (right).

because of the increased distance between the countries' capitals. The fact that the new German chancellor was cozy with Britain presented another threat to the Franco-German alliance that had long been the economic "engine" of the European Union; Schroeder had even spoken about broadening the Franco-German axis to include Britain. This irritated French President Jacques Chirac.

France and Germany have enjoyed a strong relationship since 1963, when German Chancellor Konrad Adenauer and French President Charles de Gaulle signed the Elysee Treaty, which promised that strengthened Franco-German cooperation would be "an indispensable step on the way toward a united Europe." The two countries had been the most powerful in Europe, but

Maintaining their friendship even through troubled times has been a priority for France and Germany. In this June 2001 photograph, Schroeder (right) shakes hands with French President Jacques Chirac (left) at the beginning of a summit held in Freiburg, Germany.

reunification made Germany the larger nation; and when the European Union expands to include countries of Eastern Europe, Germany will be smack-dab in the middle of Europe.

Schroeder and Chirac had certainly disagreed in the past about several aspects of European integration, like the single currency (euro). In December 2000, though, at the Nice summit, tensions had intensified between Chirac and Schroeder when

Chirac responded to Germany's call for greater voting weight in the Council of Ministers (the most powerful of the EU bodies, which handles legislative decision making) by bringing up the three German invasions of France between 1870 and 1940. As stated in *The Economist*, "the moment Germany tried to pursue its interests, even with restraint, here were dark warnings from Paris against a new German hegemony." In February 2001, Schroeder and Chirac met to patch up their differences.

The differences between the two nations were further highlighted in March 2002, when Schroeder and Blair issued a joint letter on European reform. The letter was released just before a European summit in Brussels. The joint letter was striking because before past summits, it was France and Germany that had usually drafted the joint statement. Now it was Germany and Great Britain. The letter outlined Schroeder and Blair's plan to streamline the summits, making them more efficient.

When Schroeder issued a document detailing his and Joschka Fischer's ideas for EU reform, two months later, in May, many European partners were taken aback. The report seemed to be another indication of Germany's increasing assertiveness in European affairs. The paper described a new constitution that would explain in clear language the EU's powers, along with those of national and regional governments. It also proposed a bicameral legislature—much like Germany's—that would have specific administrative and budgetary powers. It would be a powerful European superstate composed of several nation-states (like Germany and its Lander). Although the plan had many opponents, most members praised Schroeder for bringing the issue to the table. "We strongly disagree with [Schroeder]," said Francis Maude, chief foreign policy spokesman for Great Britain's Tory Party, "but at least he has the courage of his convictions." Pierre Moscovici, the French minister for Europe, said, "It's an idea that goes a long way down a German—that is to say a federalist—road. I don't think it is at the center of EU thinking."

By the end of 2002, it seemed evident that the Franco-German "engine of Europe" that had propelled the Union would never be the same again.

IMPROVING RELATIONS WITH RUSSIA

In June 2000, Russian President Vladimir Putin made an official visit to Germany, where he and his famously reclusive wife, Lyudmila, enjoyed some time with Schroeder and his wife, Doris. The four got along well, aided especially by Putin's fluency in German. (He had once been a KGB agent stationed in East Germany.) The meeting, an important one, marked the beginning of a period of improved relations between the two former enemies. Of this first visit, Putin said, "We had a sincere conversation about the problem of European security, the importance to preserve the 1972 ABM Treaty and Russia's plans to develop its politics in this very important field, and our perception of our joint participation in the activities of international organizations, including NATO and the UN."

A trip by Schroeder to Moscow in September 2000 furthered the relationship. For several hours, the two leaders discussed elections in Yugoslavia, economic ties, and Europe's oil crisis. Putin declared that Russia (one of the world's largest oil exporters) would do all it could to help Germany and Europe with fuel.

The two leaders and their wives met again in St. Petersburg, Russia, in January 2001. Putin had extended an invitation to the Schroeders to celebrate Orthodox Christmas with them. Hanging over these meetings was Russia's enormous foreign debt—$48 billion owed to Western creditors, almost half of that to Germany. Before the Schroeders visited the Putins, Russia declared that it would delay that year's first payment. German Finance Minister Hans Eichel said, "In view of the good economic situation in Russia, we expect Russia to fully meet its payment obligations. A unilateral halt to payments is not acceptable." After his meeting with Putin, Schroeder firmly stated

During his years in office, Schroeder has made efforts to develop strong ties to Russia. In September 2000, Schroder traveled to Moscow to meet with Russian President Vladimir Putin. The two leaders are seen here walking at the Kremlin in Moscow's famous Red Square.

that Russia would have to repay the money it owed—there would be no debt forgiveness. Putin relented, saying, "We intend to pay and will pay the debts of the former Soviet Union."

Although it was clear that Schroeder and Putin were getting along well, Schroeder was careful not to jeopardize Germany's loyalties to NATO and the European Union by getting too close to Russia. When he visited St. Petersburg in April 2001, he chose not to become involved in Russia's strained relations with the United States. "German foreign policy is European foreign policy," Schroeder said. "That does not mean we want to hide behind 'Europe.' But it expresses the commitment that we do exclude any German 'special way' in the relationship with Russia." Schroeder was also stern in his refusal to let Russia stall on its debt payment. When the Russians started to miss payments, Germany froze official approval for new export credit guarantees to them. Russia has since kept to all of its debt obligations.

Schroeder and Putin's strong friendship is significant, considering that Schroeder's predecessor, Helmut Kohl, focused primarily on maintaining a strong relationship with NATO and European partners. Putin has called Germany Russia's leading partner in Europe and the world. Schroeder, along with Tony Blair, has played a large role in bringing Russia closer to the West. Schroeder said, "If one looks fairly at the role Germany has played in the past 10 years, it must be said that we are the ones who carried the brunt of the weight in supporting the rebuilding of democratic structures in Russia. The dismantling of the friend-foe relationship in Europe between the West and Russia is a security improvement, and if you look at who is to be credited for this, you should find that it is Germany."

THE WAR ON TERROR IN AFGHANISTAN

On September 11, 2001, two commercial airplanes were hijacked and crashed into the two towers of the World Trade Center in New York City. Soon after, another plane rammed into the Pentagon in Washington, D.C. A fourth plane, heading to San Francisco from Newark, New Jersey, crashed in a field near Shanksville, Pennsylvania. The twin towers of the World Trade Center collapsed, parts of the Pentagon were decimated, and everyone on board each of the planes was killed. More than 3,000 people died.

As the United States and the world reeled from the horror of the events of September 11, the 19 hijackers were identified as Islamic extremists, all linked to Osama bin Laden, the fundamentalist leader of the Al Qaeda terrorist organization based in Afghanistan. President George W. Bush called for a "war on terrorism" and immediately rallied the support of an international coalition to fight terrorism. Schroeder said that he felt a "spirit of profound solidarity" with the antiterrorist coalition.

Bush demanded that Afghanistan's Taliban government, which had protected bin Laden since 1996, turn him over or the international coalition would attack. After the Taliban repeatedly refused to surrender the terrorist leader, the United States and Britain began an air campaign on October 7, targeting Al Qaeda training camps and Afghan military targets.

In early November, Schroeder offered 3,900 troops to the war against terrorism. Schroeder said that the Germans would send elite forces; armored vehicles made to detect the presence of nuclear, chemical, and biological weapons; transport planes; and medical units. The chancellor would first have to win approval from the Bundestag, though.

Political pundits commented that this represented one of most important decisions since World War II. It was a clear reminder that Germany was no longer sitting on the sidelines of the international stage. Schroeder was facing a difficult task: Although he expected his proposal to pass, many hard-line Greens and some members of the SPD strongly objected to any use of military force, urging instead a cease-fire in Afghanistan. The vice chairman of the SPD delegation, Michael Muller, said, "The fear of many is that this deployment is only the first step, and it will grow step by step."

After the terrorist attacks against the United States in September 2001, Germany expressed its support for the Americans and offered troops to take part in the war on terror. Here, Schroeder (left) and U.S. President George W. Bush (right) meet with reporters during Schroeder's visit to the White House in October 2001.

Schroeder tied the issue of troop deployment to a vote of confidence on his leadership. He even hinted that he would get rid of his coalition partners, the Greens, and replace them with the Free Democratic Party, unless they supported his plan. Joschka Fischer, who strongly supported Schroeder's proposal, warned that he would step down if his colleagues in the Green Party voted against the plan. According to Lucian Kim in the

Christian Science Monitor, Astrid Rothe, a Green Party member who opposed the deployment, said, "I think it's wrong that the coalition has been put into question. It's regrettable that Schroeder has made this link."

At the Green Party convention, Fischer delivered a rousing speech in support of the deployment and Germany's role in the fight, saying the military effort was necessary to break the cycle of terrorism. He said, "In the world of the 21st century, we cannot as a ruling party get around the military factor." Then the vote took place. Two-thirds of the delegates ultimately voted in favor of Schroeder's plan. Schroeder said that "this decision is truly important, fundamental and historic."

The immediate goal of the campaign in Afghanistan was to destroy the country's military operations and capture bin Laden. The Taliban government fell about two months after the bombing began, but bin Laden was believed to be in hiding. Bush contended, however, that "the battle is broader."

In late November, when Bush called on Iraq to allow UN weapons inspectors back into the country (as the UN required after the 1991 Persian Gulf War), it was obvious that Saddam Hussein and his regime were most likely the next intended target in the war on terrorism. Schroeder warned that the international partnership against terrorism should exercise supreme caution. "We will do everything to make sure the anti-terror coalition stays solid," he said. "We will do whatever is necessary, but reserve for ourselves the right to decide what is necessary," he said, as quoted by the BBC. He said that Germany was not "simply waiting to intervene militarily" elsewhere, and he pushed for "great restraint."

9

The Iraq Issue and Reelection

When Gerhard Schroeder entered the fourth year of his first term, his critics believed more than ever that he was a chameleon, an opportunist, a man who would switch positions and break promises (as he had on several occasions) if he thought it would ultimately make him more popular and get him reelected.

It certainly was difficult to determine where his allegiances lay, and his so-called "new middle" politics just seemed like inconsistency, which led many to question Schroeder's integrity. He had once been known as the "comrade of the bosses" for his closeness to big business, including the heads of Lufthansa and Daimler Chrysler. He was praised by German industry when he cut corporate and income tax rates, yet he occasionally seemed to show his traditional socialist roots. In November 1999, Schroeder used $129 million in taxpayer funds to rescue the construction company Philipp Holzmann from bankruptcy. He also angered industry leaders when he took actions like calling for European Commission intervention in hostile company takeovers. He said, "Hostile takeovers don't work. They cause managerial problems, they destroy value, they aren't to be welcomed." Because he was up for reelection in 2003, Schroeder seemed hesitant to make any move that might incur the anger of the highly powerful trade unions.

Internationally, the story was similar. With their shared embrace of Third Way–style politics, Schroeder and British Prime Minister Tony Blair seemed at first to have a special affinity. When they drafted their historic document in 1999, calling for more flexibility and labor reform, it seemed to signal the start of a new alliance, one that might overpower Germany's relationship with France. Schroeder's relationship with Blair, however, seemed to wither away, particularly when Schroeder worked on reestablishing positive relations with French President Jacques Chirac and Prime Minister Lionel Jospin. To his detractors, Schroeder appeared to lack conviction and simply behaved according to the polls.

THE ECONOMY

Although Schroeder had drawn praise for his tax reform package, modern immigration policy, pension plan, agreement to phase out nuclear power, and improvement of relations with Russia, these efforts were overshadowed toward the end of his first term by one major thing—the dreadful state of the economy. As Schroeder started to prepare for his reelection campaign in 2001–2002, Germany's economy was still suffering. The German unemployment rate leapt to 10.4 percent in January 2002: 4.3 million of the 41 million members of the German labor force were jobless. The nation's economy had shrunk in the last six months of 2001. Rising unemployment and the slowdown in growth, in turn, raised welfare spending and depleted tax revenues, creating a shortage in the health and pension coffers along with a budget deficit.

The terribly high unemployment rate was particularly worrisome for Schroeder, because he had declared during his first campaign that, unless he created more jobs, he would not be worthy of reelection. His much-touted "Alliance for Jobs" program, in which different groups, such as trade unions, business representatives, and government officials, tried to work together to solve the unemployment problem, ultimately failed because of the high costs of employment. To make the situation harder to repair, unemployment benefits were still about 60 to 67 percent of previous net wages, a highly attractive option for those who were out of work. Only about half of Germany's unemployed were actively seeking employment.

Critics believed that Schroeder's economic platform had not been ambitious or radical enough to truly transform the economic landscape. The extravagant social-support system in Germany was still perilously close to the breaking point. Although Schroeder was responsible for pushing through the largest tax reform package in German history, the future still looked dim for the German economy in 2002. Schroeder pinned the blame for the terrible state of the economy on global conditions.

THE CAMPAIGN, FLOODS, AND THE IRAQ CONFLICT

For several months in 2002, Schroeder and his Social Democratic Party had been lagging behind his opponent, Edmund Stoiber, a 60-year-old Bavarian representing the CDU-CSU, by six or seven points in the polls. Most voters, disappointed by the economy and unemployment, seemed to favor a new face in government.

Two events turned the election in Schroeder's favor, however. The first was heavy flooding that occurred in

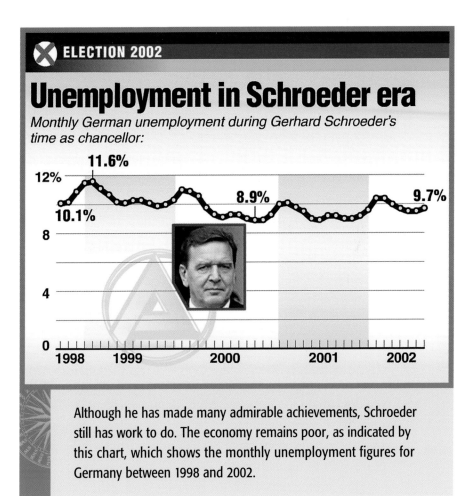

ELECTION 2002

Unemployment in Schroeder era

Monthly German unemployment during Gerhard Schroeder's time as chancellor:

11.6%

12%

10.1%

8.9%

9.7%

8

4

0

1998   1999   2000   2001   2002

Although he has made many admirable achievements, Schroeder still has work to do. The economy remains poor, as indicated by this chart, which shows the monthly unemployment figures for Germany between 1998 and 2002.

eastern Germany. In mid-August, the Elbe River and its tributaries flooded, destroying much of Saxony's heartland and other regions in the east. Schroeder smoothly handled the situation and proved himself an able and efficient crisis manager. Schroeder used his considerable gift of charm to comfort victims and proclaim his solidarity with them. He also came up with a $7 billion reconstruction plan and then deferred a tax cut for a year to cover its costs. His handling of the floods put him back in good graces with voters in eastern Germany.

The second event that provided a major surge of support

for Schroeder was the Iraq crisis. When U.S. President Bush first declared his war on terror after September 11, 2001, Schroeder expressed his "spirit of profound solidarity" with the antiterrorist coalition. Schroeder contributed troops to the effort in Afghanistan, yet expressed skepticism about Bush's plan for a broader war.

When Bush started to speak openly about the need for a "regime change" in Iraq (specifically, ousting Saddam Hussein and his government), Schroeder spoke out against it. Schroeder argued that intervention in Iraq was unjustified and that the crisis should be solved with diplomacy. When Bush lobbied the United Nations to support military action in Iraq, Schroeder rejected such action unconditionally. (The U.S. president's main reason to go to war was that Hussein was hiding weapons of mass destruction.) In a televised debate with Stoiber, Schroeder declared that Germany would not support military action in Iraq or get involved in any of Bush's "military adventures." When he expressed a similar sentiment at a campaign rally, the crowds erupted in applause. (More than 80 percent of German voters were against military intervention in Iraq.) Schroeder's approval ratings skyrocketed. His antiwar rhetoric became a central part of his platform.

This stance was incredibly risky, and other countries observed the chancellor's pronouncements against Germany's old ally, the United States, with shock. Even though most Germans are against war and have a strong pacifist streak, to oppose and even insult their country's strongest and most generous post–World War II ally was truly jarring. The tone with which Schroeder defied the American president came across to many as arrogant. (He even made it known that he had refused to take a call from President Bush, a definite slap in the face.) Many people were convinced that Schroeder was using the Iraq issue and exploiting his country's inherent antimilitarism to win the election. It seemed to be yet another glaring example of his opportunism.

Despite his earlier support for the American struggle against terrorism, Schroeder spoke out against the U.S. effort to oust Saddam Hussein's regime in Iraq. He is seen here in August 2002, addressing the media on the subject as he stands before a statue of former German Chancellor Willy Brandt.

The tension between the two world leaders grew more heated when Schroeder's justice minister, Herta Daubler-Gmelin, compared Bush to Adolf Hitler in September 2002. She said that, like "Adolf Nazi," Bush was using the war to divert Americans' attention away from their economic problems on the home-front. Condoleeza Rice, the American national security advisor, said that Schroeder had "poisoned" the German-American bond. Schroeder wrote an apology to Bush after the Hitler comparison, but it seemed to be too late. The American president felt betrayed by Schroeder.

THE ELECTION

At home, however, Schroeder's strategy to stand up to the Americans worked for him. On September 22, the SPD and the Green Party just barely won the majority of votes in the Bundestag. The race was extremely tight. With the Greens taking 8.6 percent of the vote, the Red-Green coalition had enough for a majority. Although the nation was mired in economic woes, the emotional issue of war took center stage, and won Gerhard Schroeder another term in office.

He has a very tough road ahead. Bush did not call to congratulate Schroeder on his win, although it has been customary in the past to do so. Schroeder's position (along with that of France, which also opposed the U.S. plan) on the war upset some of his EU partners. Although his moves at first appeared courageous, he ultimately looked weak. Despite his efforts, he could not prevent American military intervention in Iraq, and when that action proved exceptionally successful, many of those who had opposed it seemed to have been wrong.

Schroeder's reception at home was no better. Although he had promised no new taxes back in October, he eventually proposed increased fees and levies and fewer benefits, and Germany had to borrow more than was originally planned.

His popularity took an enormous dive, and he was even accused by Edmund Stoiber of having misled voters. Schroeder responded by saying that the true scope of Germany's financial problems had not become clear until after the election.

With the election behind him, Schroeder presses on. Part of a recent reform package included a proposal to decrease the length of time unemployed workers may claim benefits from 32 months to 12 months, and curtail laws that prevent small businesses from laying off workers. And after the "coalition forces" quickly achieved what they had set out to do in Iraq, Schroeder has decided to support a UN-backed reconstruction plan and is struggling to mend his seriously damaged relationship with the United States. Things are changing quickly in Germany. The future of German politics—and of Schroeder's career—remains to be seen.

1944 Gerhard Fritz Schroeder is born on April 7 in Mossenberg, Lower Saxony, to Fritz and Erika Schroeder; his father dies while fighting for Germany in World War II.

1951–1958 Attends elementary school.

1959–1961 Works as a retail sales assistant and an ironmonger's apprentice.

1962–1964 Attends night school and adult education courses in preparation for Abitur (to qualify for university entrance); works construction jobs.

1963 Joins Germany's Social Democratic Party (SPD).

1964 Passes his intermediate high school certificate exam.

1966 Successfully completes his Abitur.

1966–1971 Studies law at Goettingen University; works at several part-time jobs.

1968 Marries his childhood sweetheart, Eva Schubach.

1969 Becomes Young Socialists chairman in Goettingen.

1971 Divorces Schubach and marries Anne Taschenmacher.

1976 Earns law degree at Goettingen University; starts practicing law in Hanover.

1976–1978 Defends Horst Mahler, a founder of the extremist group the Red Army Faction, at his high-profile parole hearing.

1978–1980 Serves as national chairman of the Young Socialists in the SPD.

1980–1986 Serves as a member of the Bundestag for the SPD (elected from Lower Saxony).

1984 Divorces Taschenmacher; marries third wife, Hiltrud Hampel.

1986 Runs for state minister-president of Lower Saxony, but is defeated.

1986–1990 Serves as opposition leader and chairman of the SPD Group in the Lower Saxony State Parliament.

1990 **June 21** Elected minister-president of the state of Lower Saxony.

1994–1998 Reelected minister-president of Lower Saxony.

1997 Marries Doris Kopf.

1998 **March** Wins nomination as SPD candidate for chancellor at National SPD Conference.

September 27 The SPD receives 40.9 percent of the vote (and most seats in the Bundestag–298) in the general election.

October 27 Elected chancellor of the Federal Republic of Germany, ending 16 years of rule by Helmut Kohl.

1999 **January–June** Serves as president of the European Union.

March After months of tumult in the Red-Green coalition government, Oskar LaFontaine, finance minister and SPD leader, resigns from both positions; Germany contributes combat forces to NATO's effort to stop slaughter in Kosovo.

April The EU reaches an agreement on Agenda 2000.

April 12 Elected national chairman of the SPD.

2000 **June** Red-Green coalition and utility companies announce an agreement to phase out nuclear power within 25 years.

July The Bundesrat passes the most extensive tax reform package in German history; lower house of German parliament passes a bill that establishes the "Memory, Responsibility, and Future" Foundation, which compensates the Jews, Roma (gypsies), and others who were subjected to forced labor during the Nazi era.

August German government implements the "green card" program.

December German government lifts a ban that prevented immigrants and refugees from being employed in Germany; Bundesrat ratifies a law extending legal recognition to lesbian and gay partnerships.

2001 **May** The Bundesrat passes a groundbreaking pension reform bill.

September 11 Terrorists attack the World Trade Center and Pentagon in the United States; Germany pledges full support to the war on terrorism.

November Germany sends 3,900 troops to Afghanistan to participate in U.S. President George W. Bush's war on terrorism.

2002 **August** Floods ravage eastern Germany; Schroeder responds with a $7 billion aid package.

September 22 The SPD and Green coalition defeats the CDU-CSU opposition, led by Edmund Stoiber; Schroeder, whose campaign emphasized his opposition to military action in Iraq, is reelected chancellor.

October 16 Signs the second Red-Green coalition treaty.

Hancock, M. Donald. *West Germany: The Politics of Democratic Corporatism.* Chatham, NJ: Chatham House Publishers, 1989.

Krieger, Joel, ed. *Oxford Companion to the Politics of the World.* New York: Oxford University Press, 2001.

LaFontaine, Oskar. *The Heart Beats on the Left.* Cambridge, United Kingdom: Polity Press, 2000.

Meny, Yves. *Government and Politics in Western Europe: Britain, France, Italy, West Germany.* New York: Oxford University Press, 1990.

Web Sites

Bundestag Homepage:
http://www.bundestag.de/htdocs_e/index.html

CIA World Factbook, Profile of Germany:
http://www.odci.gov/cia/publications/factbook/geos/gm.html

German Embassy and German Information Center:
www.germany-info.org

German Federal Government Homepage:
http://eng.bundesregierung.de/frameset/index.jsp

page:

2: AFP/NMI
11: 21st Century Publishing
13: Reuters/NMI
17: AP/Wide World Photos
20: © Bettmann/CORBIS
23: AP/Wide World Photos
27: AP/Wide World Photos
30: © Bettmann/CORBIS
33: AP/Wide World Photos
37: AFP/NMI
42: AFP/NMI
44: AFP/NMI
50: KRT/NMI
53: AFP/NMI

56: © Bossu Regis/CORBIS SYGMA
61: AFP/NMI
63: AFP/NMI
69: AFP/NMI
71: AFP/NMI
73: EFE Photos/NMI
76: AFP/NMI
81: AFP/NMI
85: AFP/NMI
86: AFP/NMI
89: Itar-Tass Photos/NMI
92: AFP/NMI
97: KRT/NMI
99: AFP/NMI

Cover: AP/Wide World Photos

KERRY ACKER is a freelance writer and editor based in Brooklyn, New York. Among her other books for Chelsea House Publishers are MAJOR WORLD LEADERS: *Jimmy Carter*, WOMEN IN THE ARTS: *Nina Simone*, and WOMEN IN THE ARTS: *Dorothea Lange*.

ARTHUR M. SCHLESINGER, JR. is the leading American historian of our time. He won the Pulitzer Prize for his book *The Age of Jackson* (1945) and again for a chronicle of the Kennedy administration, *A Thousand Days* (1965), which also won the National Book Award. Professor Schlesinger is the Albert Schweitzer Professor of the Humanities at the City University of New York and has been involved in several other Chelsea House projects, including the series REVOLUTIONARY WAR LEADERS, COLONIAL LEADERS, and YOUR GOVERNMENT.